ST. MARY'S
ST. MARY'S CITY, MARYLAND 20686

The Luminous Ones

American University Studies

Series XXVI
Theatre Arts
Vol. 10

PETER LANG
New York · San Francisco · Bern
Frankfurt am Main · Paris · London

Elizabeth Nash

The Luminous Ones

A History of the Great Actresses

PETER LANG
New York · San Francisco · Bern
Frankfurt am Main · Paris · London

Library of Congress Cataloging-in-Publication Data

Nash, Elizabeth
   The luminous ones : a history of the great actresses /
Elizabeth Nash.
      p. cm. — (American university studies. Series
XXVI, Theatre arts ; vol. 10)
      Includes bibliographical references.
      1. Actresses—Europe—Biography. 2. Actresses—
United States—Biography. I. Title. II. Series.
PN2205.N35   1991   792'.028'09722—dc20   91-19225
ISBN 0-8204-1577-4   CIP
ISSN 0899-9880

Die Deutsche Bibliothek-CIP-Einheitsaufnahme

Nash, Elizabeth:
The luminous ones : a history of the great actresses /
Elizabeth Nash.—New York; Berlin; Bern; Frankfurt/M.;
Paris; Wien: Lang, 1991
   (American university studies : Ser. 26, Theatre arts ;
Vol. 10)
     ISBN 0-8204-1577-4
NE: American university studies / 26

The paper in this book meets the guidelines for permanence and durability
of the Committee on Production Guidelines for Book Longevity of the
Council on Library Resources.

© Peter Lang Publishing, Inc., New York 1991

All rights reserved.
Reprint or reproduction, even partially, in all forms such as microfilm,
xerography, microfiche, microcard, offset strictly prohibited.

Printed in the United States of America.

To the LUMINOUS ONES in my life

Mother   Father   Marian   James

Oscar Brockett

and

other treasured friends

ACKNOWLEDGEMENTS

"The great actors are the luminous ones."[1] The moment I read these words of the distinguished American actress Mrs. Minnie Maddern Fiske, I knew that I had found the title for a history of the great actresses.

My grateful thanks are extended to the following publishing houses and to Miss Eva Le Gallienne for permission to reprint copyright material from:

>Excerpts from *DUSE* by William Weaver, © 1984 by Thames and Hudson Ltd., reprinted by permission of Harcourt Brace Jovanovich, Inc.

>Excerpts from *The Mystic in the Theatre: ELEONORA DUSE* by Eva Le Gallienne, © 1965, 1966 by Eva Le Gallienne, reprinted by permission of Eva Le Gallienne.

---

[1] Alexander Woollcott, *Mrs. Fiske Her Views on the Stage Recorded by Alexander Woollcott* (New York: Benjamin Blom, 1968), p. 159.

CONTENTS

Preface by Maxine Greene xi
Introduction xiii
1. Antiquity to Italian Renaissance 1
2. France 1550-1803 7
3. England 1660-1831 27
4. America 1752-1876 73
5. Rachel 1821-1858 93
6. Ristori 1822-1906 115
7. Bernhardt 1844-1923 129
8. Duse 1858-1924 159
   Notes 185
   Bibliography 207
   Index 211

PREFACE

The lovely title of this text suggests the light it throws on places in art and theatre history scarcely noted before. Indeed, we knew there were great divas and great actresses; but, more often than not, we saw them through men's eyes or in the context of standard theatre histories. For too long, women—most particularly talented and beautiful women—have been viewed as occasions for appreciation by the "other," if not as objects to be flaunted and possessed. Alternatively, their efforts have been seen as decorative or incidents in male careers.

Now, because this book is written by someone who has herself performed on many stages, the truly "luminous" ones are made visible as never before. Theodora, Dumesnil, Woffington, Siddons, Duse: they have seldom broken through the pages of a tale in so much fullness, in such multidimensionality. They are not perfect; more important, they are in no way definable by means of some female "essence." Each one is distinctive; each one has a mind as well as a wondrous body. What some of them have to say about the characters they play or the scenes in which they participate adds greatly to our theatre knowledge, even as it reveals more about the women themselves. Moreover, these remarkable human beings lead their lives and play their roles in palpitant historical contexts. The chapters not only inform; they glow.

                                      Maxine Greene

                                      William F. Russell Professor
                                      Teachers College
                                      Columbia University

INTRODUCTION

The name of the famous French actress Sarah Bernhardt is well known, but what about Charlotte Cushman, Sarah Siddons, Elisa Félix, Adrienne Lecouvreur or Isabella Andreini? All made significant contributions to the theatre as the leading female performers of their respective eras. The activities of their male contemporaries are well documented, but the actresses have been sadly neglected.

This biographical history of the great actresses is intended to fill that void. As often as possible, the artists' own words have been quoted permitting them to speak for themselves. The original English translations have been used for the French and Italian actresses in order to add a flavor of the period.

CHAPTER ONE
ANTIQUITY TO ITALIAN RENAISSANCE

Theatre has been in existence for more than 2,500 years, and women have participated in this art form since its inception. Their first major theatrical roles were as tribal priestesses invoking the aid of supernatural powers for abundant harvests. Personifying fertility goddesses, they were joined in dances or dramatic rituals concerned with the seasonal cycles of birth, maturity, death, and resurrection.

Later in Egypt and Greece, acrobatic dancing girls performed in the temples, streets, and at banquets. Also in Greece, women participated in the Eleusian mysteries and the five-day Athenian Thesmorphoria honoring Demeter, goddess of agriculture. In addition, they led the orgies in honor of Dionysus, god of wine, which took place in the mountains of Thrace and Boeotia, and they sang and danced in the choral dithyrambs honoring the same god. On the isle of Crete, women toreadors performed at festivals honoring their island's Great Goddess, leaping and somersaulting over the backs of trained sacred bulls. Since these were religious ceremonies, the elegantly attired acrobats in striped loincloths, bracelets, double necklaces and ribbons round their brows were probably of the upper class. Then in Rome, women celebrated Ceres, the goddess of corn, in festivals held during the month of August.

Although women had performed in the dithyrambs, they were excluded from the tragic and comic choruses of classical Greek and Roman drama, but they did perform in the mimes, which consisted of short playlets, mimetic dances, songs, acrobatics, and juggling. These brief scenes dealt with mythological burlesques and lower-class daily life. Adultery, gluttony, beatings, thievery, and trickery were popular topics. These small mimetic troupes had been in existence from the fifth century B.C.

Women also performed in the Roman pantomimes. These storytelling solo dances were based upon historical events and myths. The artist portrayed both masculine and feminine roles with the aid of masks. The action was accompanied by an explanatory chorus and an orchestra of flutes, pipes, and cymbals. Such erotic plots as Leda and the Swan or the marriage of Dionysus and Ariadne were especially popular.

Favorite women entertainers commanded enormous fees. Several practiced their professions until more than 90 years of age. Some even had their own troupes. Many of them were noted courtesans. Cytheris was Marc Antony's mistress, and Acte was the paramour of Nero. Occasionally these women were obliged to appear naked in the Roman Floralia festival and to perform sexual acts on stage. All were social outcasts forbidden by Roman law to marry senators or their sons, and they were not allowed to renounce their professions. Later during the Christian era, these women were denied the sacraments by a church decree enacted at the Council of Carthage in 398 A.D. The Roman satirist Juvenal referred to pantomimae as "shameless." And the rhetorician Aelian stated that only a courtesan was lower than an actress in a mime. The early Christian Fathers condemned the theatre for its obscenity and for its ridicule of the church.

In 523, however, Emperor Justin's code permitted penitent actresses to marry Roman patricians if they would repudiate their profession. This statute probably resulted from the desire of Justin's nephew Justinian to marry the notorious mime and courtesan Theodora.

Knowledge of Theodora is based mainly on the *Anecdota* of the Greek historian Procopius. His pornographic description of her early life is questionable. Procopius disliked Theodora and wrote of her more than ten years after her death.

She was born early in the sixth century at Constantinople. Her father, Acacius, was bear-feeder in the amphitheatre. As a child, she performed in the mimes and became famous for her impudent acting and obscene dancing. According to Procopius,

> often before the eyes of the whole people, she stripped off her clothing and moved about naked through their midst, having only a girdle about her private parts and her groins, not, however, that she was ashamed to display these to the populace, but because no person is permitted to enter there entirely naked, but must have at least a girdle about the groins. Clothed in this manner, she sprawled out and lay on her back on the ground. And some slaves, whose duty this was, sprinkled grains of barley over her private parts, and geese, which happened to have been provided for this very purpose, picked them off with their beaks, one by one, and ate them.[2]

Theodora was a small, pale, intelligent young woman with graceful figure, beautiful features, and penetrating glance. She was noted as a courtesan and attracted the attention of Justinian. The Empress Euphemia, however, was opposed to the match. Not until her death in 523 did Emperor Justin revoke the laws of restricting actresses' marriages. Theodora then became the wife of Rome's future ruler.

Upon the death of Justin in 527, Justinian and Theodora became joint sovereigns. They resided in Constantinople, seat of the Eastern Empire, and Justinian consulted his wife on all matters of state. Oaths of allegiance were taken to the Emperor and to Theodora. Her courageous refusal to flee from the palace when under attack by rebels during the Nika Insurrection in 532 strengthened her position as co-regnant. It may have been due to Theodora's influence that the Code of Justinian limited husbands' rights to the use but not ownership or transference of their wives' properties.

As Empress, Theodora's behavior was irreproachable. Furthermore, she strictly enforced the vice laws, consigning 500 prostitutes from the streets of Constantinople to a "house of repentance" on the Bosporus. Her will was imperious. She punished those who impugned her character. Although Theodora and Justinian often differed upon affairs of state or church, it never affected their happy relationship. They had one child, a daughter. In 547, Theodora died of cancer at approximately the age of 44.

With the fall of Rome in 476, European theatre faded into oblivion. For the next 600 years, minstrels, jesters, tumblers, rope dancers, and exhibitors of trained animals roamed Europe. All were under an edict of excommunication.

By the fourteenth century, however, secular drama began to emerge. But its real impetus did not occur until the discovery in 1429 of twelve lost comedies by the Roman playwright Plautus and the appearance in the 1450's of classical Greek dramas brought to Italy by Byzantine scholars. These plays were performed in Latin, and men assumed the female roles as in Greece and Rome. Eventually, the dramas were translated into the vernacular. Allegorical playlets of songs and pantomimic dances were performed between the acts. These interludes employed female singers, dancers, jugglers, and tightrope walkers who until then had performed only in the streets and marketplaces. By the fifteenth century, the singer La

Barbera and her troupe of dancers appeared in interludes at various Italian courts. And in 1548, Italian comediennes performed at Lyons in a production of Bibbiena's *La Calandria* honoring Cathérine de Médici and Henry II.

But it was not until the appearance in the mid-sixteenth century of the *commedia dell'arte all'improviso* that women were firmly established as professional actresses. Little is known of the *commedia dell'arte's* origins. Some historians believe it can be traced to Roman Atellan farce with its rustic stock characters and coarse language. Others think it developed from Byzantine mime troupes. And there are those who contend it evolved either from improvisations on Plautus' or Terence's comedies or from early sixteenth-century Italian farce.

Improvisation and stock characters are the *commedia*'s two major characteristics. Actors performed the same characters and improvised actions and dialogue from simple plot outlines. The comedies concerned love, intrigue, disguises, and cross-purposes. There were young lovers, credulous doctors, elderly merchants, braggart soldiers, and various shrewd or naive servants.

One of the first known *commedia* actresses was Orsola Checchini, referred to as Flaminia. It was reported that her characterizations were natural and spontaneous. Vicenza Armani was another popular actress of the period. According to contemporary accounts, she was not only a superb tragic and comic actress, but also an excellent musical performer and composer. Towns saluted her arrival with cannon fire, and the nobleman Frederico de Gazuola unsuccessfully tried to abduct her.

But none compared to Isabella Andreini. Like some of her contemporaries, she was talented, beautiful, charming, graceful, and learned, but she possessed a quality which set her apart from the others -- respectability, since most of the Renaissance actresses were prostitutes.

Isabella Andreini was born at Padua in 1562. At the age of sixteen, she joined Flaminio Scala's noted *commedia dell'arte* troupe, the Gelosi. That same year she married Francesco Andreini, a fellow actor. They remained a devoted couple and had seven children.

For nearly 30 years, Isabella Andreini was the Gelosi's *prima donna innamorata*, or romantic leading lady, epitomizing the Renaissance ideal of womanly beauty, wit, and grace. She dressed in the height of fashion with brocaded silks, voluminous skirts, close-fitting bodices, neck ruffs, and jewelled caps. She also was seen to great advantage in elegant male attire for purposes of disguise.

Isabella Andreini was noted for her set pieces or appropriate speeches introduced at certain points to express emotional states of the various characters. Some actors merely memorized selections from the classics or from popular contemporary authors, but others, like Isabella Andreini, wrote their own monologues. The actress also composed two plays, *Mirtilla* and *La pazzia*.

In addition to being a superb comedienne, she was celebrated for her portrayals of Renaissance neoclassical tragic heroines. *Commedia* troupes performed both improvised comedies and written tragedies.

By 1600, Isabella Andreini was Europe's most distinguished actress. She was created laureate of Padua's Accademia degli Intenti, one of Italy's leading learned societies. The noted poet Tasso wrote sonnets praising her. Among her friends were the powerful Dukes of Mantua and Savoy.

In 1603, the Gelosi company performed in Paris at the court of Marie de Médici and Henry IV. On her way back to Italy in 1604, the actress died on June 11 in Lyons. Torch-bearing members of the city guilds escorted her coffin to a grave in sacred ground -- a rare privilege for any member of the theatrical profession. A tablet in the church bears the inscription:

"Religiosa, pia, musis amica et arti scenecae."

CHAPTER TWO
FRANCE 1550-1803

With the advent of the seventeenth century, opera became Italy's most popular theatrical entertainment. It was dominated until the 1700's by the male castrati. French actresses soon surpassed their Italian contemporaries.

For nearly 200 years, European religious drama was enacted by the clergy within the confines of the church. But by the middle of the fourteenth century, cycles of vernacular dramas based upon saints' lives and biblical characters were presented by religious guilds in the city streets and squares. Farcical scenes, along with songs and dances, featured male and female performers.

Eventually, women appeared in the mystery plays as Eve, Salome, or the Virgin, but they spoke no lines. For the most part, women were illiterate and incapable of mastering the dramas' lengthy texts. One of the first women to speak in a medieval play was an eighteen-year-old glass fitter's daughter from Metz, who performed the lead in a 1468 production of the *Mystery of St. Catherine.*

In addition to public presentations of religious dramas, Latin plays in French and Italian translations were performed at various European courts. Even women of the French royal family appeared in amateur court performances. Soon troupes of strolling players added dramas of Latin origin to their repertories which mainly consisted of farces. A contract dated 1545 is still extant between the theatrical manager Antoine l'Espéronnière and the professional actress Marie Fairet. According to its terms, she was to perform acrobatic feats and to appear in farces and Latin historical plays. In return, she would receive a nominal yearly fee in addition to room and board. Little is known of the early French actresses. They were overshadowed by their Italian rivals favored by Cathérine and Marie de Médici. Farces remained the dominant dramatic form until the appearance of neoclassical comedies and tragedies in the seventeenth century.

By that time, women had become shareholding members of their companies. Marie Vernier Laporte was a member of Valleran Le conte's troupe which performed at Paris' only permanent theatre, the Hôtel de Bourgogne. The actress performed in both tragedy and farce. She was married to a fellow actor, and upon their retirement in 1619, the couple were permitted by royal dispensation to live as citizens of Sens. Aristocratic patronage often led to a successful career in the theatre, and many actresses were the mistresses of nobleman. Thus, female performers came to be regarded as common prostitutes. Members of the court demanded admittance to the actresses' dressing rooms and even sat talking on stage during performances.

One of the early tragediennes at the Hôtel de Bourgogne was Mlle. Beauchâteau. Her affected speech and smiling countenance were satirized by Molière, who wrote: "You see how natural, how passionate that is? See how wonderfully she keeps a smiling face in the midst of the most terrible afflictions?"[1] But undoubtedly one of the most fascinating and popular actresses was Madeleine Béjart. She began her career as a tragedienne, but later was to be noted for her comic characterizations.

Madeleine Béjart, daughter of a minor government official, was born on January 8, 1618, in Paris. At an early age, she acted with various provincial touring troupes. Eventually, she established her own company entitled Les Enfants de Famille, since most of the players were relatives. In 1638, she had an illegitimate child by the Baron de Modène. Soon afterwards, she met and became the mistress of Jean-Baptiste Poquelin, son of Louis XIV's royal upholsterer. Madeleine Béjart induced this stage-struck young man to become an actor. In 1643, she and her lover, who had adopted the stage name of Molière, formed the company L'Illustre Théâtre. They opened on January 1, 1644, in a renovated indoor tennis court. For two years, the company performed tragedies starring the two partners. Although Madeleine Bejart was a successful tragedienne, Moliere was unsatisfactory in heroic roles. The troupe failed in its first Paris venture.

In 1646, the company left Paris and spent the next 12 years touring the provinces with Mlle. Béjart as leading lady and competent treasurer. This training period honed the actors' talents. They developed a natural style of speech and unconstrained movement as opposed to the old school of rant and extravagant posturing. Molière mastered his technique of comic acting, and his interest in playwriting emerged. Both were strongly influenced by his admiration of the *commedia dell'arte*.

Eventually, Madeleine Béjart was no longer able to portray the youthful heroines of tragedy or ingenues of comedy. These roles were assumed by Mlles. De Brie and Du Parc. Mlle. Béjart began performing Molière's amusing, forthright, clear-headed, practical, and strong-willed maids. The author had fashioned them after Mlle. Béjart's own personality and character. By this time, they had ceased to be lovers, but remained loyal partners and devoted friends.

In Rouen, the company was seen by Louis XIV's brother. The Duc D'Orléans arranged for their appearance before the King at the Louvre on October 24, 1658. Louis was delighted with Molière's play *Le Docteur amoureux* and the company was granted permission to perform in the theatre of the Petit Bourbon. In addition, they were to be known as the Troupe de Monsieur, the Duc D'Orléans. From then on, the company remained in Paris, competing with the comedians at the Marais theatre and the tragedians at the Hôtel de Bourgogne. In *L'Impromptu de Versailles,* Molière mocked the tragedians' bombastic speech. "Bellow the last line properly," he wrote, "That's what brings out the applause."[2]

Madeleine Béjart soon retired as the company's business manager, and the position was assumed by the efficient and handsome actor La Grange. She did, however, remain a partner and created the role of Dorine in Molière's *Tartuffe*. Béjart was intimately involved in the famous playwright's work until her death in 1672.

Madeleine Béjart was replaced in Molière's affections by her younger sister Armande. She was born in 1642 and had traveled with the company since childhood. In 1662, Molière married Armande Béjart, who was 20 years his junior. It was rumored that Armande Béjart was the daughter of Madeleine Béjart, thus suggesting that Molière had married his own child. This allegation was silenced by Louis XIV who stood as sponsor at the christening of the couple's son in 1664.

Armande Béjart had made her stage debut in 1662 as Elise in Molière's *La Critique de l'Ecole* and proved an excellent actress. This witty, independent, high-spirited, quick tongued, wayward woman became a popular artist with the Parisian public. Molière reflected Armande's qualities in the roles he wrote for her: Elmire (*Tartuffe*), Célimène (*Le Misanthrope*), Angélique (*George Dandin* and *Le Malade imaginaire*), Alcmène (*L'Amphitryon*), Armande (*Les Femmes savantes*), Elise (*L'Avare*), and Lucile (*Le Bourgeois gentilhomme*). Apparently the marriage was tempestuous, with the aging Molière seriously ill and his youthful wife at the height of her career. In 1665, after the birth of a daughter, they separated and saw each other only at the theatre. They were reconciled, however, in 1671 following Armande Béjart's appearance as Psyché in a ballet-pantomime written by Molière, Corneille, and Phillippe Quinault. The actress gave birth to a son one year later.

By now, Molière was dying of tuberculosis. On February 17, 1673, Armande Béjart pleaded with her husband to cancel his performance of Argan in *Le Malade imaginaire*. During the last act, Molière had a seizure and died several hours later. The church refused extreme unction to the distinguished actor and playwright. When Christian burial was also denied Molière by the Archbishop of Paris, his wife appealed to Louis XIV. Throwing herself at his feet, the actress exclaimed that if her husband's theatrical activities were considered to be excommunicable, they indeed had been sanctioned by the King himself. Louis intervened, and Molière's body was buried in St. Joseph's cemetery on February 21. The interment took place at night without a funeral service. A protesting mob outside Molière's home was appeased by the widow throwing golden coins out of the window. The coffin was accompanied to the burial ground by Molière's friends bearing torches.

Armande Béjart was not a good businesswoman and allowed La Grange to manage her husband's troupe. In 1673, the company merged with the Marais troupe.

Molière's widow married the actor François Guérin and continued to act until 1694. She died on November 30, 1700, and was buried two days later at the church of Saint-Sulpice. As prototypes and originators of Molière's fascinating female characters, the two Béjarts left a rich legacy.

During the second half of the seventeenth century, France's leading tragediennes were Mlles. Desoeillets, Du Parc, and Champmeslé. Mlle. Desoeillets was born in 1621. She performed in the provinces until 1660 when she joined the Marais troupe in Paris. By 1662, she had moved to the Hôtel de Bourgogne and remained there until her death in 1670. Despite her lack of youth or good looks, she became a leading performer, noted for her moving performances of Corneille's and Racine's tragic heroines.

The beautiful and haughty Marquise-Thérèse Du Parc was born in 1633. For many years she was a member of Molière's troupe and performed the role of Arsinoé in Moliere's comedy *Le Misanthrope*. It was as a tragedienne, however, that she excelled.

In 1664 and 1665, Molière produced two of Racine's tragedies. Racine was dissatisfied with the second production. From then on his plays were presented at the Hôtel de Bourgogne. Mlle. Du Parc had become his mistress. In 1666 or 1667, he induced her to desert Molière's company and join the troupe at the Hôtel de Bourgogne.

During the season of 1667, Mlle. Du Parc created Racine's *Andromaque*. Supposedly, the playwright coached her on both lines and gestures. Soon she became the Bourgogne's leading actress, but her career was brief. In 1668, she died either in childbirth or from the aftereffects of an abortion. Eleven years later, the notorious sorceress Cathérine Montvoisin asserted at her trial for murder and witchcraft that Mlle. Du Parc had been poisoned by Racine out of jealousy. The allegation has never been proved.

Mlle. Du Parc's successor at the Hôtel de Bourgogne and as Racine's mistress was Marie Champmeslé. She was the wife of the actor-playwright Charles Chevillet, known as Champmeslé. The actress was born of good family in 1642 at Rouen. She was a provincial actress until 1669, when she made her Paris debut at the Marais theatre as Vénus in Boyer's *Fête de Vénus*.

Within six months, she had moved to the Bourgogne and became the uncontested queen of French tragedy. In 1670, Mlle. Champmeslé performed with such brilliance the role of Hermione in Racine's *Andromaque* that Mlle. Desoeillets, who had created the part in 1667, exclaimed: "Desoeillets is no more."[3]

Mlle. Champmeslé's reputation was established. Racine wrote for her the roles of Bérénice, Roxanne (*Bajazet*), Iphigénie, and finally Phèdre. As with Mlle. Du Parc, Racine tutored his new mistress in her roles. She was praised by her contemporaries for the naturalness of her acting, the exceptional beauty of her voice, and her superb declamatory style in contrast to the stilted performances of her predecessors.

Mlle. Champmeslé also was noted for her portrayals of Pierre Corneille's heroines, Chimène (*Le Cid*) and Camille (*Horace*). And she was praised for her performances of Thomas Corneille's Elisabeth I (*Le Comte d'Essex*) and Ariane. In the latter she made her debut as a member of La Grange's troupe. Mlle. Champmeslé and her husband had joined this company in 1679. The actress had been lured away from the Hôtel de Bourgogne by La Grange's offer of an annuity and two shares in the company's receipts.

Thus the Bourgogne had lost its leading tragic actress and her actor-playwright husband. To avoid a major theatrical crisis, Louis XIV ordered the merger of Paris' two rival companies. In 1680, the Comédie Française was established as Europe's first national theatre. The company opened on August 26 with a performance of *Phèdre*, starring Mlle. Champmeslé.

In addition to her popularity as an actress, Mlle. Champmeslé was a noted hostess. France's most distinguished literary artists frequented her salon. Racine was often a guest at her receptions, as were the poet and critic Nicolas Boileau-Despréaux and also Jean de La Fontaine, author of the famous *Fables*. La Fontaine dedicated his novel *Belphegor* to her.

Mlle. Champmeslé continued to be France's leading actress until her death on May 15, 1698. On her deathbed she had renounced her profession and received the last rites. Her body was buried at Saint-Sulpice.

Mlle. Champmeslé was succeeded at the Comédie Française by her niece and pupil Charlotte Desmares. Like her aunt, Mlle. Desmares was praised for her declamation and naturalness. She won acclaim for the tragic roles of Racine's Hermione (*Andromaque*) and Athalie as well as for Corneille's Jocaste (*Oedipe*) and Emilie (*Cinna*). Also she was an excellent comedienne. Until her retirement in 1721, she was France's most popular actress.

Mlle. Desmare's rival at the Comédie Française was Marie-Anne Duclos, understudy and student of Mlle. Champmeslé. This period saw a revival of the former artificial, highly emotional, and bombastically oratorical style of acting. Despite her realistic training, Mlle. Duclos became a representative of this mode.

Her most successful roles were Corneille's Ariane and Antoine Houdard de La Motte's Ines de Castro. One evening during a performance of La Motte's tragedy, the audience in the pit laughed when Mlle. Duclos as the doomed Spanish heroine entered with her two children in the last act. Highly incensed, the actress swept down to the footlights. In solemn tones, she angrily addressed the ladies and gentlemen of the court: "Just laugh, foolish parterre, just laugh at the most touching place in the play."4 Rather than resenting her audacious behavior, the aristocratic audience responded with applause. The performance concluded without further interruption.

Mlle. Duclos remained at the Comédie Française until 1736. But for the last 16 years of her career, she was overshadowed by one of the most famous actresses in the history of the French stage Adrienne Lecouvreur.

Adrienne Lecouvreur was born on April 5, 1692, at Damery in Champagne. She was the daughter of a hat maker, who moved to Paris in 1702. At the age of 15, she performed tragedies and comedies with a group of young people in a grocer's shop. Because of the youthful actress' successful portrayal of Pauline in Corneille's *Polyeute*, the amateur company was invited to appear at the home of wealthy and fashionable Mme. Lejay. After only one presentation, the lieutenant of police ordered them to cease, since the Comédie Française had been granted a monopoly on all spoken drama in French. The young players moved to the district of the Temple outside the jurisdiction of the Paris police. There they performed *Polyeute* until the troupe disbanded because of quarrels among its members.

Adrienne Lecouvreur studied acting with Le Grand, a member of the Comédie Française. In 1708, he procured an engagement for her in the provinces. For nine years, she performed in Lille, Luneville, Metz, Nancy, Verdun, and Strasbourg. In 1717, she was offered an engagement at the Comédie Française. She made her debut as Prosper Jolyot Crébillon's Electre.

The naturalness and simplicity of her diction compared to the stilted enunciation and almost chant-like delivery of her contemporaries delighted the Paris public. Unlike Mlle. Duclos, whose formal presentation of verse was considered to be overly emphatic and rhythmical, Adrienne Lecouvreur spoke her lines with emphasis on content rather than on rhyme. Her dignified yet simple gestures matched her delivery, and her voice, although limited in range, was used to express a rich variety of emotions. She was noted for the excellence of her pantomime, and her keen imagination enlivened her characterizations. Although some thought her acting lacked dignity, Adrienne Lecouvreur soon was acknowledged to be France's leading actress. Mlle. Duclos was regarded as old-fashioned.

Mlle. Lecouvreur excelled in the tragedies of Racine and Corneille. But she also was a competent comedienne, performing the roles of Molière's Célimène (*Le Misanthrope*) and Elmire (*Tartuffe*). She especially was noted for her performance of Ines de Castro, and she originated Voltaire's heroines Artémire and Mariamne. At first, Voltaire disapproved of her delivery which de-emphasized the metrical composition of his verse. Eventually, however, he came to esteem her as the finest actress in the history of French theatre.

In addition to her professional triumphs, Adrienne Lecouvreur was socially popular. She was natural in manner, intelligent, witty, spirited, graceful, refined, tactful, and noble in disposition. These qualities contributed to her acceptance in court circles. Her receptions were eagerly attended by literary, military, and administrative notables in addition to ladies of high rank who normally avoided an actress' society.

Mlle. Lecouvreur never encouraged her wealthy and aristocratic admirers to lavish their fortunes on her. This may have led to her social acceptability among women of the court. The young Comte d'Argental was passionately in love with her. His mother Mme. Ferriol, fearing that her son might marry the famous actress, threatened to send him to St. Domingo in the West Indies. Hearing of this plan, Adrienne Lecouvreur wrote the following letter to the distraught mother:

Paris, March 22, 1721

Madame,

It is not without great pain that I learn of your anxiety and of the plans you are making as a result. I have been equally grieved I might add to hear that you blame my conduct; but I am writing to you less to justify it than to protest to you that, in the future, in all that is of interest to you, it shall be such as you may wish to prescribe. Tuesday I had asked permission to see you in order to speak to you in confidence and to ask for your commands. But your manner of receiving me destroyed my zeal and I found myself only timid and sad in your presence. It is necessary, however, that you should know my true sentiments, and, if you will allow me to add, that you should not disdain to hear my very humble remonstrances, if you do not wish to lose your son.

He is the most respectful, the most honorable young man I have ever met in my life. How you would admire him if he were not a part of you! Once again, Madame, deign to join with me in destroying the weakness which irritates you, but in which I have no part, whatever you may say. Do not be bitter or scornful toward him. In spite of the tender friendship, and the veneration I hold for him, I would rather take upon myself all his hatred, than expose him to the least temptation which might cause him to lose his respect for you. You are too much interested in curing him not to be anxious to attain your objective. But your very eagerness makes you unable to attain it alone, especially when you seek to put an end to his love by an attitude of authority, or by painting me in a disadvantageous light, whether true or not. This passion must surely be extraordinary, since it has existed so long a time without hope, in the midst of disappointments, in spite of the voyages you have made him undertake, and of eight months' stay in Paris without seeing me—at least not at my house—and when he had no reason to believe I should ever receive him again. I thought he was cured, and therefore consented to see him during my last illness. It is easy to believe that seeing him would give me infinite pleasure were it not for this unhappy passion, which astonishes as much as it flatters me, and of which I refuse to take advantage. You fear that by seeing me he will forget his duties, and you push this fear to the point of making violent decisions against him. In truth, Madame, it is not just that he be rendered unhappy in so many ways. Do not add to my own severity toward him; seek rather to lighten his burden. Make all his resentment fall upon me, but let him find consolation in your kindness.

I will write to him whatever you please; I will never see him again if you desire it; I will even go away into the country if you deem it necessary. But do not threaten to send him to the end of the world. He could be useful to his country; he will be the delight of his friends; he will fill you with satisfaction and cover you with glory; you only have to guide his talents and let his virtues act for themselves. Forget for a while that you are his mother, if maternity is in any way opposed to the kindness which, on my knees, I beg you to show him. Finally, Madame, I would rather retire from the world, or love him out of passion, than allow that he be further tormented for or by me. Grant your forgiveness to a feeling which you can destroy, but upon which I can have no effect. Add what I now beg of you to all the other acts of kindness you have bestowed upon me, and allow me to think that my sincere attachment and my lively gratitude will make you keep for me the kindly feeling which I so value; and permit me to congratulate myself throughout life on being, with profound respect, Madame, your very humble and very obedient servant,

>   Adrienne Lecouvreur.

P.S. Let me know what you wish me to do. If you desire to speak to me without his knowing it, I will meet you wherever you please, Madame, and will spare no pains, no efforts, in order that you may be satisfied with both your son and me.[5]

The relationship ended, and Mlle. Lecouvreur soon became the mistress of the handsome, dashing, and debauched Maréchal Maurice de Saxe, illegitimate son of King Augustus II of Poland. De Saxe was one of France's most brilliant generals, and in 1725, Adrienne Lecouvreur sold her jewels and plate to finance his campaign in Courland. After his return to France in 1728, Maurice de Saxe had tired of the distinguished actress and sought out other mistresses. Adrienne Lecouvreur was furious at his infidelities. Seeing her former lover enter the auditorium during a performance of *Phèdre*, she snatched a sword from her fellow actor's hand and threw it at de Saxe.

At another performance of *Phèdre*, Adrienne Lecouvreur saw de Saxe's latest mistress the Duchesse de Bouillon seated in a box. With telling emphasis, she directed toward her the lines: "I know my baseness. O, I am not like those brazen women who, tasting in theirs sins a peace serene, dare flaunt a face where not a blush is seen."[6] Soon after, the Duchesse attempted to murder the actress with a gift of poisoned lozenges. The frightened messenger, however, had been advised by his confessor to inform Mlle. Lecouvreur of their content.

In mid-March, Adrienne Lecouvreur suddenly was taken ill during a performance of Voltaire's *Oedipe*. Her health had always been fragile. After four days of agony, she died in the arms of Voltaire. It was rumored that she had been poisoned by the Duchesse de Bouillon who had visited the actress in her dressing room shortly before her collapse. An autopsy arranged by Voltaire showed that her death had been caused by ulceration of the bowels.

Adrienne Lecouvreur had died without renouncing her profession. The Archbishop of Paris forbade her burial in consecrated ground. Late at night her body was placed in a carriage. Accompanied by a police officer, it was driven to a barren area near the Seine. France's greatest actress was cast into a hastily dug grave with quicklime for a pall.

In striking contrast, the popular London actress Anne Oldfield was buried seven months later in Westminster Abbey. Voltaire composed a scathing elegy comparing the ignominious interment of Adrienne Lecouvreur to that of her English colleague. He never forgot the indignity of Lecouvreur's burial. Nearly 30 years later he wrote: "She was refused what people here call 'decent burial,' in other words, the right to rot in a foul graveyard along with the local paupers. She was buried alone and friendless at the corner of Burgundy Street, which must have grieved her exceedingly, for she had very high ideals."[7]

Adrienne Lecouvreur was followed at the Comédie Française by two rival actresses, Marie Françoise Dumesnil and Claire-Josèphe-Hippolyte Clairon. Mlle. Dumesnil was born on January 2, 1713, in Paris of a poor but respectable Norman family. In 1733, she began acting at theaters in eastern France. She made her debut at the Comédie Française in 1737 as Clytemnestra in Racine's *Iphigénie*. Soon she distinguished herself as Phèdre, Cléopâtre (Corneille's *Rodogune*), Elisabeth (*Le Comte d'Essex*), and Hilaire Bernard de Roqueleyne Longpierre's Medea. She excelled in violently emotional tragic characterizations.

It is reported that when she moved downstage to deliver some fearful curse, those in the pit recoiled spontaneously. In 1742-43, Mlle. Dumesnil was cast as Voltaire's Mérope. The rehearsals were conducted by the playwright. Voltaire was a demanding director. When the actress informed him that "to act as you wish, I should need to have a devil in me," he replied, "Precisely; to excell in any art one must be possessed of a devil."8 She apparently fulfilled Voltaire's demands because he later claimed that the drama's success was due to Mlle. Dumesnil's acting. In the fourth act, she was roundly applauded for running from the wings instead of moving with the traditional measured tread of the tragic heroine.

In 1736, Mlle. Dumesnil created Voltaire's Sémiramis. Her costume as Assyria's sovereign closely resembled the Queen of France's gown of state. Like her predecessors, she favored contemporary splendor to historical accuracy.

Mlle. Dumesnil's acting was erratic. She depended upon inspiration rather than technique. She believed that "to imbue oneself with great emotions, to feel them immediately and at will, to forget oneself in a twinkling of an eye in order to put oneself in the place of the character one wishes to represent—that is exclusively a gift of nature and beyond all the efforts of art."9 Denis Diderot, the eighteenth-century philosopher and man of letters, wrote of her acting, "Half the time she does not know what she is saying: but she has one sublime moment."10 The quality of her portrayals depended upon the depth of her emotional involvement at the moment.

At the age of 63, she retired from the Comédie Française and lived in modest circumstances until her death on February 20, 1803.

Mlle. Dumesnil's rival at the Comédie Française was Claire-Josèphe-Hippolyte Clairon, the illegitimate daughter of an army sergeant and a seamstress. Born in Condé on January 25, 1723, Mlle. Clairon and her mother eventually moved to Paris. At the age of 11, Mlle. Clairon became fascinated with the stage. The young girl would stand at a window carefully observing her neighbor Marie-Anne Dangeville of the Comédie Française taking dancing lessons. She then would imitate the actress' movements. Clairon informed her mother that she was "determined to be an actress."[11] The ill-natured seamstress viewed the stage as "the road to eternal damnation."[12] Despite many blows, Clairon remained adamant, declaring, "Well, you may kill me if you please; but, for all that, I will be an actress."[13] Finally her mother relented and allowed Clairon to be tutored by the actor Deshais. He obtained an engagement for his pupil at the Comédie Italienne.

In 1736, Clairon made her debut as a soubrette. Soon after, she accepted a contract in Rouen and performed as a juvenile utility actress, singer of comic opera, and ballet dancer. Following several years in the provinces, she sang the role of Vénus in André Campra's *Hesione* at the Paris Opera. A few months later she was engaged at the Comédie Française to serve as Mlle. Dangeville's understudy. Mlle. Clairon chose the role of Racine's Phèdre for her debut on September 19, 1743. Soon she rivaled Mlle. Dumesnil.

The two performers were artistic antitheses. Mlle. Dumesnil, like Adrienne Lecouvreur, had renounced the artificial formalism of the early eighteenth century in favor of naturalness. Mlle. Clairon, on the other hand, was declamatory in style, although not so exaggerated as Mlle. Duclos. The acting of Mlle. Dumesnil was noted for its emotionality, while that of Mlle. Clairon was marked by a subtly hidden control. Mlle. Clairon carefully rehearsed her roles, memorizing every gesture and intonation. Her movements and declamation were measured and stately. An admirer of her studied effects, Diderot acclaimed Mlle. Clairon as the greatest actress of her age. But David Garrick, England's most famous eighteenth century actor, wrote:

> She has everything that Art and a good understanding, with great Natural Spirit can give her--But I fear--the Heart has none of those instantaneous feelings, that Life blood, that keen Sensibility, that bursts at once from Genius, and like Electrical fire shoots thro' the Veins, Marrow, Bones and all, of every Spectator. --Madm Clairon is so conscious and certain of what she can do, that she never (I believe) had the feelings of the instant come upon her unexpectedly.[14]

Later in her career, upon the advice of the critic and playwright Jean François Marmontel, Mlle. Clairon simplified her declamatory style. She assumed a more natural, conversational delivery. In keeping with this change, she adopted relatively historical costumes. "In all my characters the costume must now be observed;" she claimed, "the truth of declamation requires that of dress."[15] In the role of Voltaire's Electre *(Oreste),* she appeared in an unpretentious black gown instead of wearing the traditional voluminous hooped mourning robe. Her hair was dishevelled and her arms weighed down by long chains. In Voltaire's *L'Orphelin de la Chine,* she wore pantaloons rather than the large paniered skirts favored by Mlle. Dumesnil.

Mlle. Clairon was noted for her performances of Racine's Phedre, Hermione, Iphigénie, and Monime *(Mithridate).* Of the latter, the actress wrote:

> Monime is one of the most edifying and moving roles that exist in the theatre...but it is also one of the most difficult. Without shouts and outbursts of passion, without the excuse for striding up and down the stage, for having determined gestures, and for using varied and impressive facial acting,

it seems impossible to save the role from its initial appearance of monotony. While such techniques would benefit the actress, they would scarcely be suited to the role.16

Also she was famous for her portrayals of Crébillon's Electre and Zénobie, as well as Longpierre's Medea. And she created Voltaire's Electre, Idame (*L'Orphelin de la Chine*), and Amenaide (*Tancrède*).

The elegant, ambitious, imperious, high-spirited and dissolute Mlle. Clairon is said to have had 25 wealthy lovers, several of whom she ruined financially. Often they were only means to further her career or to maintain a luxurious life style. According to one writer: "Life came to her in two great passions—love of art and love of man; she sacrificed all else for these, and occasions never came in her life when she found herself obliged to choose between them."17

Suddenly in 1766, Mlle. Clairon retired from the Comédie Française. A fellow actor named Dubois had cheated on a doctor's bill. Indignant at her colleague's chicanery, Clairon obtained his expulsion from the Comédie Française. The Duc de Fronsac was an admirer of Dubois' daughter and had the actor reinstated. Mlle. Clairon and four of her fellow actors refused to appear with him in Pierre Laurent Buirette De Belloy's *Le Siège de Calais*. The actress and her associates were incarcerated in Fort L'Evêque, a royal prison for persons under administrative order. As servants of the King, they were subject to imprisonment for failure to observe royal commands. Mlle. Clairon spent five days in a luxuriantly furnished cell, receiving visitors, and presiding over sumptuous supper parties. She was permitted to return home because of "ill health," although some suggested social exhaustion. Mlle. Clairon and her four colleagues adamantly refused to perform with

Dubois, and he was retired with full pension.

Clairon soon left the Comédie Française, claiming ill health and fear of perdition. The actress long had protested the ecclesiastical ban of excommunication placed upon the theatrical profession.

Mlle. Clairon opened a school of acting in Paris. Then in 1773, she moved to Germany with her lover, the Margrave of Anspach. Eighteen years later, the Margrave married the Countess of Craven. Mlle. Clairon returned to Paris and died in 1803, at the age of 80.

CHAPTER THREE
ENGLAND 1660-1831

Unlike the acting troupes of Italy and France, which had numbered women among their members since the mid-sixteenth century, professional actresses did not appear upon the English stage until 1656. Until that time, all female dramatic roles were performed by men. There were, however, women dancers, singers, acrobats, and minstrels. Women also took part in the May Day games, the Morris dances, and in religious dramas. The women of medieval Chester produced and may have performed in the pageant of the Assumption of the Virgin.

The English were scandalized at the mere thought of women exhibiting themselves in public. The Puritans regarded it as an abomination. The idea of women appearing on stage was so offensive to the London public that in 1629, the female members of a visiting French troupe were hissed and pippin-pelted at the Blackfriars Theatre.

During the reigns of James I and Charles I, women of the royal family sometimes were seen in elegant pageants or masques as was customary in France. Courtiers were familiar with the appearance of women on stage because many had seen French and Italian actresses abroad.

With the advent of Puritan rule in 1642, all theatrical performances were banned. Even the celebration of Christmas was outlawed in 1647. In September 1656, however, Mrs. Coleman, wife of the composer Edward Coleman, performed the part of Ianthe in the first English opera, *The*

Siege of Rhodes. It was produced by Sir William D'Avenant in his theatre at Rutland House. Mrs. Coleman sang her role with score in hand.

When the monarchy was restored in 1660, Charles II established duopolistic royal patent theatres in London. The King's Company was under the direction of Thomas Killigrew, and the Duke of York's Company was managed by Sir William D'Avenant. Charles and his cavaliers were avid theatre-goers. During their exile on the Continent, they had learned to prefer actresses to female impersonators. The King authorized the employment of actresses, claiming that some people were offended at female parts being performed "by men in the habit of women." He also argued that the introduction of actresses might "by such reformation be esteemed not onely harmless delight, but useful and instructive representation of human life."[1] Charles wisely instituted the appearance of actresses under the guise of moral reform. Formerly, zealots had decried the employment of women performers. Now they maintained that the appearance of female impersonators tended to encourage homosexuality.

Although Mrs. Coleman probably was the first English woman to appear on the London stage, she was an amateur performer. Thus in 1660, either Mary Saunderson or Anne Marshall was the first professional English actress.

Aside from their names, little is known of many early English actresses. Like their French counterparts, English actresses were officially servants of the king. Since the Restoration theatre was fundamentally a diversion for the licentious Charles and his lascivious court, many penniless young women found the theatre a method of acquiring wealthy lovers. English aristocrats also visited the actresses in their dressing rooms and considered them little better than harlots. Therefore, by the end of Charles' reign in 1685, female players generally were regarded as "kept women."

This was not true, however, of Mary Saunderson Betterton, England's first leading professional actress. Her reputation was impeccable. Nothing is known of Mary Saunderson's childhood except that she was born around 1637. Probably in 1660, she joined the Duke of York's Company. She was one of four actresses living in the home of Sir William D'Avenant, who undoubtedly trained them for the stage.

In June 1661, Mary Saunderson very likely made her debut as Ianthe in parts one and two of D'Avenant's *The Siege of Rhodes*. Two months later, she was the first woman to perform the role of Shakespeare's Ophelia (*Hamlet*). Her leading man was the distinguished actor Thomas Betterton, whom she married in December 1662. Until his death in 1710, they remained a devoted couple.

Aside from being the first female Ophelia, Mrs. Betterton also was the first woman to perform Juliet, Lady Macbeth, Queen Katherine (*Henry VIII*), Beatrice (*Much Ado About Nothing*), Viola (*Twelfth Night*), Isabella (*Measure for Measure*) and perhaps Cordelia (*King Lear*). According to the famous actor-playwright Colley Cibber, she excelled in Shakespearean roles and was as Lady Macbeth "so great a Mistress of Nature" that she could "throw out those quick and careless Strokes of Terror from the Disorder of a guilty Mind,...with a Facility in her Manner that rendered them at once tremendous and delightful."[2] Apparently her actions were relatively free from stylized exaggeration and her speech from bombast. In addition, her range was extensive, including tragedy, comedy, farce, and opera. She was equally successful as John Webster's tormented Duchess of Malfi or John Dryden's roguishly coquette Elvira in *The Spanish Friar*. During her 30 years on the stage, she was the originator of 25 roles, including Bellinda (Sir George Etherege's *The Man of Mode*), Jocasta (Dryden's *Oedipus*), and Lady Leycock (Thomas Betterton's *The*

Amorous Widow).

Mary Betterton was a court favorite noted for both her diction and her virtue. In 1675, she was selected to coach the Princesses Mary and Anne for roles in a court masque. Later both Queens were praised for their clear voices and graceful enunciation. Queen Anne granted her former teacher a pension, but it was never paid.

Towards the end of her career, Mrs. Betterton played older parts such as the Duchess of York in Shakespeare's *Richard III*. She also trained young actresses for the stage, one of whom was Anne Bracegirdle. In 1693, Mary Betterton retired from the theatre. On April 13, 1712, she was buried beside her famous actor husband in the Cloisters of Westminster Abbey.

The Restoration period in England was an era of extreme sexual license. Thus the virtuous life of Mary Betterton contrasted strikingly with that of the notorious, witty, and fascinating Nell Gwyn. Born on February 2, 1650, in the London slum of Coal Yard, Nell Gwyn was the daughter of a drunken prostitute. As a child, she sold fish and vegetables in the streets around Drury Lane and Covent Garden. By the age of 13, she was engaged as a serving wench in Madam Ross' Lewknor Lane brothel. Later Mary Meggs hired her to sell oranges to the gentlemen patrons in the pit of Killigrew's Theatre Royal. She was popular with Charles' courtiers for her quick wit and bawdy banter. Soon she became the mistress of Charles Hart, leading actor of the King's Company and formerly a female impersonator. Hart probably taught her to read, act, and dance the jig for which she became famous.

In November 1664, Nell Gwyn made her debut as the courtesan Paulina in Killigrew's *Thomaso*. There followed other minor parts until the theatres were closed by plague in May 1665. Shortly after the reopening of the Theatre Royal in February 1667, Nell Gwyn scored a resounding success in Dryden's *Secret Love* as the brazen and impudent

Florimel. At the play's conclusion, the actress danced a saucy jig attired in breeches, hat, coat, and periwig of a swaggering Restoration buck. This madcap role was ideally suited to Nell Gwyn's flamboyant personality and graceful figure. Samuel Pepys wrote of her: "But so great a performance of a comical part was never, I believe in the world before as Nell do this, both as a mad girle, then most and best of all when she comes in like a young gallant; and hath the motions and carriage of a spark the most that ever I saw any man have."[3] Because of her success as Florimel, she often was cast in breeches' parts.

Although her forte was high-spirited hoydens in ribald comedy, she also performed tragic roles. She disliked serious parts, admitting to her own inadequacies as a tragedienne. Dryden added a comic epilogue to *Tyrannic Love* in which the corpse of the lovesick, suicidal Valeria sat up in her bier complaining over the "damn'd dull poet, who could prove so senseless, to make Nelly die for Love."[4] Then with a sly wink and kiss of the hand, she again lay down and was borne off stage amid general laughter and applause. Pepys concurred with Nell Gwyn's appraisal of her dramatic talent, writing: "Nell's and Hart's mad parts are most excellently done, but especially her's; which makes it a miracle to me to think how ill she do any serious part, as, the other day, just like a fool or a changeling; and, in a mad part, do beyond all imitation almost."[5]

For a short time after her affair with Charles Hart had ended, she was the mistress of Charles Sackville, Earl of Dorset. Then in 1669, she began her permanent liaison with Charles II, who wittily referred to himself as Nell's Charles III. Following the birth of her first son by the King, Nell Gwyn retired from the stage to live in luxury as a royal mistress. She also was lady of the Queen's Bedchamber.

Although there were numerous rivals for Charles' affections, Nell Gwyn remained popular with the libidinous Monarch, who enjoyed her wit and good nature. She always was able to amuse him. Her bedwarmer was inscribed: "Fear God, and serve the King." On one occasion, after her rival the Duchess of Cleveland had been seen in a carriage drawn by an eight--instead of the customary six--horse team, Nell Gwyn appeared in a coach pulled by eight oxen. She never attempted to conceal her humble origins. When an antipapist mob in Oxford attacked her carriage, mistaking it for that of the Catholic Duchess of Portsmouth, the former actress called out: "Pray, good people, be civil; I am the Protestant whore!"[6] The populace cheered and permitted her carriage to pass.

Charles died in 1685. Nell Gwyn survived him by only two years, succumbing on November 14, 1687, to apoplexy. The bulk of her considerable estate was left to her one surviving son, the Duke of St. Albans. She stipulated, however, that £100 be spent for clothing the poor in wintertime and for freeing the poverty-stricken from debtors' prison. Nell Gwyn was buried in the crypt of St. Martin's-in-the-Fields despite the objection of numerous communicants. The Vicar Dr. Thomas Tenison pronounced the eulogy at her funeral and insisted upon her interment in his own vault. This tolerant churchman later became Archbishop of Canterbury. Although her stage career lasted for only seven years, her scintillating personality and notorious life style established her as the most famous actress of the Restoration era.

Nell Gwyn's colleague, the distinguished actress Elizabeth Barry, was equally promiscuous. Born in 1648, she was the daughter of an impoverished barrister. Elizabeth Barry was raised and educated by her father's friends, the William D'Avenants.

In September 1675, she made an unsuccessful debut as Draxilla in Thomas Otway's *Alcibiades* at the Dorset Garden Theatre. Soon she was dismissed from the Duke's Company. According to the notorious eighteenth-century publisher Edmund Curll, the Earl of Rochester wagered that he could teach Elizabeth Barry to act in six months. She became his pupil and mistress. Supposedly Rochester taught her to "enter into the Nature of each Sentiment; perfectly changing herself, as it were, into the Person, not merely by the proper Stress or Sounding of the Voice, but feeling really, and being in the Humor, the Person she represented, was supposed to be in."[7]

Mrs. Barry was re-engaged by the Duke's Company in 1676. The following year, she gave birth to a daughter by Lord Rochester. Early in 1680, the actress won distinction as the original Monimia in Otway's *The Orphan*. Two years later she created one of her greatest roles Belvidera in the premiere of Otway's *Venice Preserved*.

Since her debut in 1675, Elizabeth Barry had made rapid strides as an actress. Whether her improvement was a result of Rochester's coaching or of her own intelligence and diligence is unknown.

In 1682, the King's and Duke's Companies were merged and became the United Company. Mrs. Barry was England's acknowledged leading lady. Four years later, she was permitted to retain one evening's box office receipts each season, thus instituting the tradition of actors' benefit performances. Mrs. Barry jealously guarded her financial and artistic prerogatives. For a performance of Nathaniel Lee's *The Rival Queens*, she was denied the use of an elegant veil favored by tragediennes of the day. That right had been granted to her colleague Elizabeth Boutell. In the play's murder scene, the enraged actress stabbed her colleague so violently that the blunted dagger passed through her rival's corset and entered her flesh.

Belligerent and independent, Elizabeth Barry joined with Thomas Betterton to form their own company in 1694. They were dissatisfied with Christopher Rich's management. The new company was under the joint direction of Betterton and Mrs. Barry. She and her colleague Anne

Bracegirdle became the first English female theatrical shareholders.

In April, the company opened with William Congreve's *Love for Love* with Elizabeth Barry as Mrs. Fainall. Then on March 5, 1700, she created the role of Mrs. Marwood in Congreve's *The Way of the World*. Although she was an excellent comedienne, she excelled in tragedy and in 1703 appeared as Calista in the first performance of Nicholas Rowe's *The Fair Penitent*.

In 1700, Mrs. Barry surrendered her youthful roles to Anne Bracegirdle. Until her retirement in 1710, she performed the roles of Gertrude (*Hamlet*), Queen Katherine (*Henry VIII*), Mrs. Ford (*The Merry Wives of Windsor*), and Lady Macbeth. Colley Cibber claimed that her portrayal of the Scottish queen was inferior to that of Mrs. Betterton's.

According to Thomas Betterton, Mrs. Barry took infinite care in preparing her roles and even "...so exerted herself in an indifferent Part, that her Acting has given success to such Plays, as to read would turn a Man's Stomach."[8] Regarding the realism of her acting, Betterton stated: "She indeed always enters into her Part, and is the Person she represents."[9] In tragedy her bearing was commanding and regal, while in comedy she was noted for ease of manner and fluid variety of gesture. Cibber wrote of her voice that it was "full, clear, and strong, so that no Violence of Passion could be too much for her: and when Distress or Tenderness possess'd her, she subdued into the most affecting Melody and Softness."[10] She was praised for the variety and normalcy of her facial expressions. Like Betterton, there was a naturalness to her acting. She avoided posturing, rant, or excessive quaver in the voice. Mrs. Barry radiated a sense of beauty and voluptuousness despite her lack of good looks.

Her final public performance was on June 13, 1710, as Lady Easy in Cibber's *The Careless Husband*. On November 7, 1713, she died of hydrophobia at her home in Acton. She had been bitten by a favorite lap dog. In her will, Mrs. Barry left more than £200 to her friend and theatrical successor, Anne Bracegirdle.

Daughter of a Northampton innkeeper or coach maker, Anne Bracegirdle was born in 1663. Because of her father's financial losses, she was brought up by his friends' Thomas and Mary Betterton who trained her for the stage. In 1680, she may have performed the part of the page Cordelio in Otway's *The Orphan*. Her official debut was on February 6, 1688, as Atelina in the United Company's production of William Mountfort's *The Lovers*.

For the next two years she performed such ingenue roles as the Indian Queen in Aphra Behn's *The Widow Ranter*. By 1690, she appeared as the tragic heroines Statira (*The Rival Queens*), Desdemona (*Othello*), and Queen Anne (*Richard III*). In 1702, she added Ophelia (*Hamlet*) to her repertoire of Shakespearean roles. Rowe wrote for her the parts of Lavinia (*The Fair Penitent*) and Selima (*Tamerlane*).

Although Anne Bracegirdle was successful in tragedy, she excelled in comedy, creating the sophisticated heroines of Congreve's plays. In March 1693, she performed the role of Araminta in Congreve's first play *The Old Bachelor*. This was followed in April 1695, by Angelica (*Love for Love*), and then Millamant (*The Way of the World*) in March 1700. Congreve's heroines epitomized the seventeenth-century female ideal of elegance, coquetry, and genuine affection.

Anne Bracegirdle was celebrated for her portrayals of virtuous women whom she endowed with a subtle alluring sexuality. She was known as "the Celebrated Virgin" and the "Diana of the Stage." In tribute to her chastity, a group of noblemen presented her with 800 guineas.

Aloof to admirers, she returned Lord Burlington's present of china, suggesting that an error obviously had been made, since it undoubtedly was a gift for his wife. Mrs. Bracegirdle zealously guarded her reputation. But it is rumored that she had been the mistress of Congreve and later of Robert Leke, Earl of Scarsdale.

Perhaps the competition of the rising young actress Anne Oldfield prompted Mrs. Bracegirdle to retire from the stage in 1707 at the height of her popularity. It is reported that the two actresses on successive evenings performed the role of Mrs. Brittle in Betterton's *The Amorous Widow*. The youthful Anne Oldfield's portrayal was judged superior.

For the next 40 years, Mrs. Bracegirdle lived in comfort and social respectability. She numbered among her friends Horace Walpole, Earl of Oxford. Her interest in the theatre never waned, and occasionally she attended a performance. When Cibber criticized the new star David Garrick, she commented: "Come, come, Cibber, tell me if there is not something like envy in your character of this young gentlemen. The actor who pleases everybody must be a man of merit."[12] The generous, discreet, and charming Anne Bracegirdle died on September 12, 1748, and was buried in the Cloisters of Westminster Abbey.

Mrs. Bracegirdle's competitor, the beautiful Anne Oldfield, was the daughter of an unsuccessful London innkeeper turned soldier who died soon after her birth in 1683. She first earned her living as a seamstress and then as a barmaid. During leisure moments at her aunt's tavern, she read aloud to herself from plays. At the age of 16, she was overheard by the dramatist George Farquhar. Impressed by her talent, Farquhar recommended her to his colleague and friend Captain John Vanbrugh. He in turn introduced her to Christopher Rich, manager of the Drury Lane Theatre. Rich, noted for his parsimony, hired her for fifteen shillings a week. For nearly four years, she made little impression on either her fellow players or the public.

However, upon the death of the actress Susanna Verbruggen in 1703, Anne Oldfield inherited the part of Leonora in John Crown's *Sir*

Courtly Nice. Colley Cibber was featured in the leading role. Cibber was unimpressed by the young actress who muttered her lines in resentment at his indifference during the rehearsal. On the night of the performance, Cibber was amazed at her transformation. "So forward and sudden Step into Nature I had never seen;" he wrote, "and what made her Performance more valuable was that I knew it all proceeded from her own Understanding, untaught and unassisted by any one more experienced Actor."[13]

One year later, Anne Oldfield was cast as the beautiful and fashionable Lady Betty Modish in Cibber's new play *The Careless Husband.* She was an instant success. During the next three years, she added the roles of Celia (Ben Jonson's *Volpone*), Monimia (*The Orphan*), and Florimel (Cibber's *The Comical Lovers*).

She created Silvia in Farquhar's *The Recruiting Officer* and Mrs. Sullen in his *The Beaux' Stratagem.* Dressed in breeches as Silvia, Anne Oldfield delighted the beaux in the audience with her tall, well-proportioned figure, and elegant carriage. She also amused them with her witty renderings of Mrs. Sullen's suggestive repartee.

By 1709 Mrs. Oldfield was out of patience with Christopher Rich's niggardly management of Drury Lane. She joined Colley Cibber, Robert Wilks, Owen Swiney, and Thomas Dogget in forming a company at the Queen's Theatre, Haymarket. They were to have been partners, but Dogget objected claiming the theatre's "affairs could never be upon a secure Foundation, if there was more, than one Sex admitted to the Management of them."[14] Instead of a share, Mrs. Oldfield received £200 a year and an expense-free benefit performance. In 1711, however, the Queen's Theatre became an opera house. Anne Oldfield returned to Drury Lane, where she remained for the next 19 years.

With the retirement of Mrs. Bracegirdle in 1707, Anne Oldfield was unrivaled in high comedy. She long had professed an antipathy to tragedy stating: "I hate to have a Page dragging my Tail about."[15] Mrs. Oldfield was referring to the tragedienne's obligatory train borne by pages. Soon, however, she began appearing in tragedies. After her success in Lee's *Mithridates*, she launched forth as a tragic actress in 1708. She created the roles of Andromache (Ambrose Philips' *The Distrest Mother*), Marcia (Joseph Addison's *Cato*), Rowe's Jane Shore and Lady Jane Gray. Later she appeared as Calista (Rowe's *The Fair Penitent*), Margaret (*Henry VI, Part 2*), and James Thomson's Sophonisba.

Mrs. Oldfield was noted for grace and elegance of movement as well as for beauty and strength of voice. Her diction was impeccable. Voltaire claimed she was the only English actress whom he could easily understand. In addition, she always strove to improve her acting. Unlike many of her contemporaries, she readily welcomed suggestions. "Her excellence in acting, " wrote Cibber, "was never at a stand...by knowing so much herself, she found how much more there was of Nature yet to be known. Yet it is a hard matter to give her any Hint that she was not able to take or improve."[16]

Cibber later commented that even at the age of 45 Mrs. Oldfield "outdid her usual Excellence"[17] when she created the role of Lady Townley in his comedy *The Provoked Husband*. At the premiere, a member of the audience hissed as the actress began to speak the epilogue. With a scornful look, she paused and then interjected the words: "poor creature." Immediately the audience burst into applause, and Mrs. Oldfield brought the play to its conclusion.

Anne Oldfield was not only England's most popular actress but also an accepted member of London society and a leader of fashion. Sir Richard Steele referred to her as "ever well-dressed" and "the genteelest woman"[18] of her day. Cibber wrote of her performance as Lady Betty

Modish that "Had her Birth placed her in a higher Rank of Life she had certainly appeared in reality what in this Play she only excellently acted, an agreeably gay Woman of Quality."[19] Perhaps her liaison with the sophisticated Sir Arthur Maynwaring fostered her elegance of manner and superb taste in dress, furnishings, paintings, and sculpture. The cultured actress was later admitted to court circles as the mistress of Colonel Charles Churchill, the illegitimate nephew of the Duke of Marlborough.

In the mid-1720's, Anne Oldfield developed cancer. She retired from the stage in April 1730, following a performance of Lady Brute in Vanbrugh's *The Provoked Wife*. Realizing that death was at hand, she refused to accept any salary from Drury Lane during the last two months of her life. On October 22, 1730, the still beautiful Anne Oldfield died at the age of 47. Her devoted maid and dresser Betty prepared her mistress for burial in a linen shift, Brussels lace ruffles and cap, and new kid gloves. After lying in state for a day in Westminster Abbey's Jerusalem Chamber, her body was buried in the Abbey. No monument was allowed to be erected in her honor, but the actress rests interred next to a former dean of the Abbey.

Anne Oldfield was succeeded on the London stage by Hannah Pritchard and Margaret Woffington. The first to challenge memories of Mrs. Oldfield at Drury Lane was Hannah Pritchard, the daughter of a strolling player named Vaughn. She was born in 1711 and by the age of 22 had performed the role of Loveit in *A Cure for Covetousness or The Cheats of Scapin* at Fielding and Hippisley's theatrical booth in Bartholemew Fair.

Following performances in 1733, Mrs. Pritchard was engaged to perform comic roles at the Haymarket. Then in 1734, she transferred to Drury Lane. At first she was confined to minor comic parts, but in 1736, she attained fame as Rosalind (*As You Like It*) and later as Beatrice (*Much Ado About Nothing*), Lady Betty Modish (*The Careless Husband*), Mrs. Sullen (*The Beaux' Stratagem*) and Lady Brute (*The Provoked Wife*). Soon, however, she turned to tragedy and performed Shakespeare's Anne Boleyn (*Henry VIII*), Lady Macduff (*Macbeth*), Desdemona (*Othello*), and Lady Anne (*Richard III*). During the 1740's, she added to her repertoire the roles of Jane Shore, Belvidera (*Venice Preserved*), Calista (*The Fair Penitent*), Mrs. Beverley (Moore's *The Gamester*), Volumnia (*Coriolanus*), Gertrude (*Hamlet*), and Lady Macbeth. The latter was regarded as her finest role, although Samuel Johnson claimed she never had read the entire play. Thomas Davies, a contemporary biographer, wrote of her sleepwalking scene: "Pritchard's acting resembled those sudden flashes of lightning which more accurately discover the horrors of surrounding darkness."[20] In 1749, she created the leading female role in Samuel Johnson's unsuccessful tragedy *Mahomet and Irene*. At the premiere, the indignant audience refused to witness the heroine's strangulation on stage. "Murder! Murder!" they cried! Mrs. Pritchard was led to her death in the wings.

Her portrayals were characterized by naturalness of speech and action, as was also true of David Garrick, her frequent leading man and manager of Drury Lane from 1747 till 1776. Both eschewed early eighteenth-century stylized posturing, the "toned" declamation of the French school, or the monotonic rhyming of the English. The old style was represented by Mrs. Pritchard's colleague Susanna Arne Cibber, a former singer. According to contemporary accounts, she literally sang or "recitatived" her lines, wearying the listener with the boring uniformity of her intonation. Mrs. Cibber had been taught by her father-in-law, Colley Cibber, to "tone" her words while Mrs. Pritchard had rejected his advice. According to a contemporary viewer, Hannah Pritchard completely submerged her own personality. "Nothing of herself appears," he claimed, "but all the characters."[21] Samuel Johnson observed that in private she was a "vulgar idiot" who referred to her "gownd", while on stage she "seemed to be inspired by gentility and understanding."[22]

Often she was deeply affected by the emotions of her roles and "fell in fits behind the scenes."[23] This strong emotional identification with a portrayal was evidenced in her performance of Gertrude during the closet scene in *Hamlet*. When she was asked by her son if she saw the ghost, "She turned her head slowly round, and with a certain glare in her eyes, which looked everywhere and saw nothing, spoke the line, 'Nothing at all; yet all that's here I see!'"[24]

Mrs. Pritchard led a circumspect life as the wife of William Pritchard, treasurer of Drury Lane. They had numerous children. In April 1768, she retired from the stage. Only four months later she died of a gangrenous foot infection. A white marble tablet honoring her was erected in the Poets' Corner of Westminster Abbey. Perhaps an even greater tribute to her artistry was David Garrick's refusal to perform *Macbeth* without her.

Mrs. Oldfield's other successor on the English stage was the fascinating Margaret Woffington. On November 21, 1740, the actress took London by storm as Sir Harry Wildair in Farquhar's *The Constant Couple*. The daughter of an Irish bricklayer, Peg Woffington was born in 1717. At an early age, she sang ballads and sold watercress in the streets of Dublin to aid her widowed mother. Around 12 years of age, she joined the Lilliputians, a children's company managed by Madame Violante, a French rope dancer. The young girl was taught acting and dancing. The French performer also instructed her in diction and singing to correct her pronunciation and a harshness of voice which was to plague the actress throughout her career. She was featured as Polly Peachum and later Macheath in a production of John Gay's *The Beggar's Opera*.

After several successful seasons, Madame Violante took her company to London in 1732 for two weeks of performances at The Haymarket. The London audiences, however, did not favor the youthful performers. Margaret Woffington returned to Dublin where in 1734, she was engaged as an entr'acte dancer at the Theatre Royal, Aungier Street.

The playwright Charles Coffey encouraged her to develop a facility with language through reading of books in both English and French, the latter of which she had learned from Madame Violante. In addition, she attended rehearsals and performances to view other actresses' portrayals of fashionable ladies. She also observed women of quality in the audience.

In 1736, after replacing an indisposed actress as Shakespeare's Ophelia, Peg Woffington became a regular member of the Aungier Street company. During the next four years, she performed the roles of the flirtatious maid Phillis (Sir Richard Steele's *The Conscious Lovers*) and the swaggering, male-attired Silvia (*The Recruiting Officer*). Then in 1740, she won acclaim as the first female performer of the high-spirited, debonair, and rakish Sir Harry Wildair. The beauty of her tall, supple, well-proportioned figure attired in a gleaming satin suit, combined with her grace of movement and buoyant radiance, caught the popular fancy.

Following performances of *The Constant Couple*, Margaret Woffington was besieged by admiring aristocrats. Among them was a handsome young man named Taafe, the son of an impoverished Irish peer. She soon became his mistress. Although he spoke of marriage, Taafe's engagement to an heiress eventually became known to Peg Woffington. According to legend, the irate actress donned male garb and devised an introduction to the intended bride at a ball. She showed her Taafe's love letters to Peg Woffington, and the young woman broke her engagement.

Perhaps her unhappy love affair or Ireland's serious economic vicissitudes led Peg Woffington to seek employment at London's Covent

Garden in 1740. She was refused admittance to the home of manager John Rich eighteen times. Finally, on her nineteenth attempt, she was granted entry. Dazzled by her beauty, Rich engaged her immediately. Her debut on November 6, 1740, as Silvia was a success. Fifteen days later, she took London by storm as Sir Harry Wildair. *The Constant Couple* was performed 20 times during the season. No male performer could rival her in that role. "She repeated it," recorded the actor Tate Wilkinson, "with never ceasing applause for several years."[25]

Despite Margaret Woffington's success, Rich rejected her demand for an increase in salary. Thus in 1741, she signed a contract at Drury Lane. For the next seven years she performed her ever-popular Silvia and Sir Harry Wildair, in addition to Lady Brute (*The Provoked Wife*), Mrs. Sullen (*The Beaux' Stratagem*), Nerissa (*The Merchant of Venice*), Rosalind (*As You Like It*), and Cordelia (*King Lear*).

Aside from her fame as an actress, Peg Woffington was a popular hostess. Her receptions were attended by Samuel Johnson and by Fanny Burney, a novelist and letter writer. The actress introduced her sister Polly to London society following completion of her education at a French convent. The attractive, well mannered, and intelligent young woman married the penniless aristocrat Captain Robert Cholmondeley. Margaret Woffington granted them a stipend. Lord Cholmondeley objected to his son's alliance with a player's sister, until Peg Woffington retorted that she was really the offended party, now having two beggars to support instead of one!

Peg Woffington was not only beautiful but also intelligent, and had cultivated a graceful, distinguished manner. Admired by men of position and intellect, she was described by Johnson as "dangerously seductive."[26] She may have had numerous affairs, but she genuinely loved David Garrick with whom she lived and shared household expenses from 1742 until 1744. On the day of their marriage, Garrick was morose and hesitant. Margaret Woffington cancelled the wedding and left him. She masked her emotions, but Garrick attacked her in a bitter poetic diatribe describing her various liaisons.

In his capacity as partial manager of Drury Lane, he maliciously cast her in supporting parts while assigning her well-known roles to other actresses. Jealous of Margaret Woffington's beauty and fame, Susanna Cibber, Hannah Pritchard, and the sharp-tongued comedienne Kitty Clive baited their good-natured colleague. She usually parried their barbs with witty sarcasm. On one occasion, however, Kitty Clive managed to ruffle her equanimity. While portraying the part of Lady Percy in a performance of Shakespeare's *Henry the Fourth*, she became enraged at Kitty Clive's taunting expressions of sympathy for having to appear in minor roles. The two women shouted and struck at each other back stage until separated by the actor Spranger Barry.

Artistically stymied, Margaret Woffington terminated her engagement at Drury Lane in April 1748. She spent the summer studying acting with the noted French tragedienne Marie Dumesnil. Peg Woffington's portrayals of tragic roles had been marred by her use of stylized movements and rhythmical intoning of lines. According to Mlle. Dumesnil, speech and movement were external manifestations of the character's inner nature. She taught the English actress naturalness and flexibility of voice emanating from the lines' emotional content. This aided in alleviating Peg Woffington's stridency of tone, especially noticeable in tragic verse drama. Although she never fully overcame her vocal harshness, Margaret Woffington developed more vocal control. This aided her in attaining popular if not critical acclaim for portrayals of Jane Shore, Calista (*The Fair Penitent*), and Andromache (*The Distrest Mother*).

But Peg Woffington was never to excel in tragedy. Comedy remained her forte. Her beauty, vivacity, majestic grace and sheer magnetism were ideally suited to the roles of the fashionable Lady Townley (*The Provoked Husband*), Lady Betty Modish (*The Careless Husband*), and Millamant (*The Way of the World*). Also her fine figure continued to be an advantage in breeches' parts.

Margaret Woffington was re-engaged at Covent Garden in 1748. She remained there until 1751, when she accepted an engagement at Dublin's Theatre Royal, Smock Alley. From 1751 until 1754, she dominated Ireland's theatrical scene. In addition, she was the sole female member and later president of the exclusive Beefsteak Club, which met once a week for dinner and conversation.

In 1754, she returned to Covent Garden. On May 17, 1757, she was stricken with paralysis while performing the role of Rosalind. This final performance was described by Tate Wilkinson:

> She went through Rosalind for four acts without my perceiving she was in the least disordered, but in the fifth she complained of great indisposition....When she came off at the quick change of dress, she again complained of being ill; but got accoutered and returned to finish the part, and pronounced in the epilogue speech, "If it be true that good wine needs no bush, it is as true that a good play needs no epilogue," etc. etc. - But when arrived at - "If I were among you I would kiss as many of you as had beards that pleased me." - her voice broke, she faltered, endeavoured to go on, but could not proceed - then in a voice of tremor screamed; O God! O God! tottered to the stage-door, speechless, where she was caught.[28]

For the next three years, she lingered broken in health and died on March 26, 1760. Her body was interred in the parish church at Teddington.

Two years before Margaret Woffington's collapse at Covent Garden, the greatest actress in the annals of the British stage was born on July 5, 1755, at the Shoulder of Mutton Inn in Brecon, Wales. Sarah Kemble was one of twelve children born to the strolling players Robert and Sarah Kemble. The couple managed a troupe of thirteen men and women. Travelling from town to town, they appeared in barns, inn yards, and occasionally theatres. They often referred to their productions as musical concerts. The Licensing Act of 1737 forbade the performance of legitimate drama for "gain, hire or reward" without permission of the Lord Chamberlain. They were in constant danger of arrest under the Vagrancy Act of 1713, which denied legal status to strolling players. They were classed as rogues and vagabonds.

Sarah Kemble attended various schools in towns visited by her parents' troupe. The young child was taught singing and declamation by her mother. Sarah Kemble was a voracious reader. By the age of ten she was a devotee of Milton's poetry.

On November 25, 1773, she married William Siddons, a handsome but mediocre member of the Kemble's troupe. In 1774, the youthful couple joined the touring company of Chamberlain and Crumb. Mrs. Siddons was cast in the leading roles of Otway's Belvidera (*Venice Preserved*), Shakespeare's Rosalind (*As You Like It*), and Lady Macbeth. The part of Lady Macbeth had a profound influence upon the 20 year old actress. She later recounted:

> It was my custom to study my characters at night, when all the domestic cares and business of the day were over. On the night preceding that in which I was to appear in this

part for the first time, I shut myself up as usual, when all the family were retired, and commenced my study of Lady Macbeth. As the character is very short, I thought I should soon accomplish it. Being then only twenty years of age, I believed, as many others do believe, that little more was necessary than to get the words into my head, for the necessity of discrimination, and the development of character, at that time of my life, had scarcely entered into my imagination. But to proceed. I went on with tolerable composure, in the silence of the night (a night I never can forget), till I came to the assassination scene, when the horrors of the scene rose to a degree that made it impossible for me to get farther. I snatched up my candle, and hurried out of the room in a paroxysm of terror. My dress was of silk, and the rustling of it, as I ascended the stairs to go to bed, seemed to my panic-struck fancy like the movement of a spectre pursuing me. At last I reached my chamber, where I found my husband fast asleep. I clapt my candlestick down upon the table, without the power of putting the candle out, and I threw myself on my bed, without daring to stay even to take off my clothes. At peep of day I rose to resume my task; but so little did I know of my part when I appeared in it at night, that my shame and confusion cured me of procrastinating my business for the remainder of my life.[29]

Mrs. Siddons later was to make fascinating observations on the character of Lady Macbeth:

In this astonishing creature one sees a woman in whose

bosom the passion of ambition has almost obliterated all the characteristics of human nature; in whose composition are associated all the subjugating powers of intellect and all the charms and graces of personal beauty. You will probably not agree with me as to the character of that beauty; yet, perhaps, this difference of opinion will be entirely attributable to the difficulty of your imagination disengaging itself from that idea of the person of her representative which you have been so long accustomed to contemplate. According to my notion, it is of that character which I believe is generally allowed to be most captivating to the other sex,—fair, feminine, nay, perhaps, even fragile—

'Fair as the forms that, wove in Fancy's loom, Float in light visions round the poet's head.'

Such a combination only, respectable in energy and strength of mind, and captivating in feminine loveliness, could have composed a charm of such potency as to fascinate the mind of a hero so dauntless, a character so amiable, so honourable as *Macbeth*,—to seduce him to brave all the dangers of the present and all the terrors of a future world; and we are constrained, even whilst we abhor his crimes, to pity the infatuated victim of such a thraldom. His letters, which have informed her of the predictions of those preternatural beings who accosted him on the heath, have lighted up into daring and desperate determinations all those pernicious slumbering fires which the enemy of man is ever watchful to awaken in the bosoms of his unwary victims. To his direful suggestions she is so far from offering the least opposition, as not only to yield up her soul to them, but moreover to invoke the sightless ministers of remorseless cruelty to extinguish in her breast all those compunctious visitings of nature which otherwise might have been mercifully interposed to counteract, and perhaps eventually to overcome, their unholy instigations. But having impiously delivered herself up to the excitements of hell, the pitifulness of heaven itself is withdrawn from her, and she is abandoned to the guidance of the demons whom she has invoked.

Here I cannot resist a little digression, to observe how sweetly contrasted with the conduct of this splendid fiend is that of the noble single-minded *Banquo*. He, when under the same species of temptation, having been alarmed, as it appears, by some wicked suggestions of the *Weird Sisters*, in his last night's dream, puts up an earnest prayer to heaven to have these cursed thoughts restrained in him, *'which nature gives way to in repose.'* Yes, even as to that time when he is not accountable either for their access or continuance, he remembers the precept, 'Keep thy heart with all diligence; for out of it are the issues of life.'

To return to the subject, *Lady Macbeth*, thus adorned with every fascination of mind and person, enters for the first time, reading a part of one of those portentous letters from her husband. 'They met me in the day of success; and I have learnt by the perfectest report they have more in them than mortal knowledge. When I burnt with desire to question them further, they made themselves into thin air, into which they vanished. Whilst I stood wrapt in the wonder of it, came missives from the King, who all hailed me 'Thane of Cawdor,' by which title before these Sisters had saluted me, and referred me to the coming on of time with '*Hail, King that shall be!*' This I have thought good to deliver thee, my dearest partner of greatness, that thou mightst not lose the dues of rejoicing, by being ignorant of what greatness is promised. Lay it to thy heart, and farewell.' Now vaulting ambition and intrepid daring rekindle in a moment all the splendours of her dark blue eyes. She fatally resolves that *Glamis* and *Cawdor* shall be also that which the mysterious agents of the Evil One have promised. She then proceeds to the investigation of her husband's character:

   'Yet I do fear thy nature,
It is too full of the milk of human kindness
To catch the nearest way. Thou wouldst be great,
Art not without ambition, but without
The illness should attend it. What thou wouldst highly,
That thou wouldst holily. Wouldst not play false,
And yet wouldst wrongly win. Thou'dst have great
  Glamis,
That which cries, *Thus thou must do if thou have it!*
And that which rather thou dost fear to do
Than wishest should be undone.'

In this development, we find that, though ambitious, he is yet amiable, conscientious, nay pious; and yet of a temper so irresolute and fluctuating, as to require all the efforts, all the excitement, which her uncontrollable spirit, and her unbounded influence over him, can perform. She continues—

'Hie thee hither,
That I may pour my spirits in thine ear,
And chastise with the valour of my tongue
All that impedes thee from the golden round,
Which fate and metaphysical aid doth seem
To have thee crown'd withal.'

Shortly *Macbeth* appears. He announces the King's approach; and she, insensible it should seem to all the perils which he has encountered in battle, and to all the happiness of his safe return to her,—for not one kind word of greeting or congratulation does she offer,—is so entirely swallowed up by the horrible design, which has probably been suggested to her by his letters, as to have entirely forgotten both the one and the other. It is very remarkable that *Macbeth* is frequent in expressions of tenderness to his wife, while she never betrays one symptom of affection towards him, till, in the fiery furnace of affliction, her iron heart is melted down to softness. For the present she flies to welcome the venerable gracious *Duncan*, with such a shew of eagerness, as if allegiance in her bosom sat crowned with devotion and gratitude.

"*The Second Act.*

There can be no doubt that *Macbeth*, in the first instance, suggested his design of assassinating the king, and it is probable that he has invited his gracious sovereign to his castle, in order the more speedily and expeditiously to realize those thoughts, *'whose murder, though but yet fantastical, so shook his single state of man.'* Yet, on the arrival of the amiable monarch who had so honoured him of late, his naturally benevolent and good feelings resume their wonted power. He then solemnly communes with his heart, and after much powerful reasoning upon the danger of the undertaking, calling to mind that *Duncan* his king, of the mildest virtues, and his kinsman, lay as his guest. All those accumulated determents, with the violated rights of sacred hospitality bringing up the rear, rising all at once in terrible array to his awakened conscience, he relinquishes the atrocious purpose, and wisely determines to proceed no further in the business. But, now, behold his evil genius, his grave-charm, appears, and by the force of her revilings, her contemptuous taunts, and, above all, by her opprobrious aspersion of cowardice, chases the gathering drops of humanity from his eyes, and drives before her impetuous and destructive career all those kindly charities, those impressions of loyalty, and pity, and gratitude, which, but the moment before, had taken full possession of his mind. She says,

'I have given suck, and know
How tender 'tis to love the babe that milks me.

I would, while it was smiling in my face,
Have pluck'd my nipple from its boneless gums,
And dash'd the brains out,—had I but so sworn
As you have done to this.'

Even here, horrific as she is, she shews herself made by ambition but not by nature, a perfectly savage creature. The very use of such a tender allusion in the midst of her dreadful language, persuades one unequivocally that she has really felt the maternal yearnings of a mother towards her babe, and that she considered this action the most enormous that ever required the strength of human nerves for its perpetration. Her language to *Macbeth* is the most potently eloquent that guilt could use. It is only in soliloquy that she invokes the powers of hell to unsex her. To her husband she avows, and the naturalness of her language makes us believe her, that she had felt the instinct of filial as well as maternal love. But she makes her very virtues the means of a taunt to her lord:—'You have the milk of human kindness in your heart,' she says (in substance) to him, 'but ambition, which is my ruling passion, would be also yours if you had courage. With a hankering desire to suppress, if you could, all your weaknesses of sympathy, you are too cowardly to will the deed, and can only dare to wish it. You speak of sympathies and feelings. I too have felt with a tenderness which your sex cannot know; but I am resolute in my ambition to trample on all that obstructs my way to a crown. Look to me, and be ashamed of your weakness.' Abashed, perhaps, to find his own courage humbled before this unimaginable instance of female fortitude, he at last screws up his courage to the sticking-place, and binds up each corporal agent to his terrible feat. It is the dead of night. The gracious *Duncan*, now shut up in measureless content, reposes sweetly, while the restless spirit of the wickedness resolves that he shall wake no more. The daring fiend, whose pernicious potions have stupified his attendants, and who even laid their daggers ready,—her own spirit, as it seems, exalted by the power of wine,—proceeds, 'That which hath made them drunk hath made me bold,' now enters the gallery, in eager expectation of the results of her diabolical diligence. In the tremendous suspense of these moments, while she recollects her habitual humanity, one trait of tender feeling is expressed, 'Had he not resembled my father as he slept, I had done it.' Her humanity vanishes, however, in the same instant; for when she observes that *Macbeth*, in the terror and confusion of his faculties, has brought the daggers from the place where they had agreed they should remain for the crimination of the grooms, she exhorts him to return with them to that place, and to smear those attendants of the sovereign with blood. He, shuddering, exclaims, 'I'll go no more! I am affear'd to think of what I have done. Look on't again I dare not.'

Then instantaneously the solitary particle of her human feeling is swallowed up in her remorseless ambition, and, wrenching the daggers from the feeble grasp of her husband, she finishes the act which the infirm of purpose had not courage to complete, and calmly and steadily returns to her accomplice with the fiend-like boast,

> 'My hands are of your colour;
> But I would scorn to wear a heart so white.'

"A knocking at the gate interrupts this terrific dialogue; and all that now occupies her mind is urging him to wash his hands and put on his nightgown, *'lest occasion call,'* says she, *'and shew us to be the watchers.'* In a deplorable depravation of all rational knowledge, and lost to every recollection except that of his enormous guilt, she hurries him away to their own chamber.

"*The Third Act.*

The golden round of royalty now crowns her brow, and royal robes enfold her form; but the peace that passeth all understanding is lost to her for ever, and the worm that never dies already gnaws her heart.

> 'Nought's had—all's spent,
> *Where our desire is had without content.*
> *'Tis safer to be that which we destroy,*
> *Than by destruction dwell in doubtful joy.'*

Under the impression of her present wretchedness, I, from this moment, have always assumed the dejection of countenance and manners which I thought accordant to such a state of mind; and, though the author of this sublime composition has not, it must be acknowledged, given any direction whatever to authorize this assumption, yet I venture to hope that he would not have disapproved of it. It is evident, indeed, by her conduct in the scene which succeeds the mournful soliloquy, that she is no longer the presumptuous, the determined creature, that she was before the assassination of the King: for instance, on the approach of her husband, we behold for the first time striking indications of sensibility, nay, tenderness and sympathy; and I think this conduct is nobly followed up by her during the whole of their subsequent eventful intercourse. It is evident, I think, that the sad and new experience of affliction has subdued the insolence of her pride, and the violence of her will; for she comes now to seek him out, that she may, at least, participate his misery. She knows, by her own woful experience, the torment which he undergoes, and endeavours to alleviate his sufferings by the following inefficient reasonings:

'How now, my lord—why do you keep alone?
Of sorriest fancies your companions making?
Using those thoughts which should indeed have died
With them they think on. Things without all remedy
Should be without regard. What's done, is done.'

"Far from her former habits of reproach and contemptuous taunting, you perceive that she now listens to his complaints with sympathizing feelings; and, so far from adding to the weight of his affliction the burthen of her own, she endeavors to conceal it from him with the most delicate and unremitting attention. But it is in vain; as we may observe in his beautiful and mournful dialogue with the physician on the subject of his cureless malady: 'Canst thou not minister to a mind diseased?' &c. You now hear no more of her chidings and reproaches. No; all her thoughts are now directed to divert his from those sorriest fancies, by turning them to the approaching banquet, in exhorting him to conciliate the goodwill and good thoughts of his guests, by receiving them with a disengaged air, and cordial, bright, and jovial demeanour. Yes; smothering her sufferings in the deepest recesses of her own wretched bosom, we cannot but perceive that she devotes herself entirely to the effort of supporting him.

Let it be here recollected, as some palliation of her former very different deportment, she had, probably, from childhood commanded all around her with a high hand; had uninterruptedly, perhaps, in that splendid station, enjoyed all that wealth, all that nature had to bestow; that she had, possibly, no directors, no controllers, and that in womanhood her fascinated lord had never once opposed her inclinations. But now her new-born relentings, under the rod of chastisement, prompt her to make palpable efforts in order to support the spirits of her weaker, and, I must say, more selfish husband. Yes; in gratitude for his unbounded affection, and in commiseration of his sufferings, she suppresses the anguish of her heart, even while that anguish is precipitating her into the grave which at this moment is yawning to receive her.

"*The Banquet.*

Surrounded by their court, in all the apparent ease and self-complacency of which their wretched souls are destitute, they are now seated at the royal banquet; and although, through the greater part of this scene, *Lady Macbeth* affects to resume her wonted domination over her husband, yet, notwithstanding all this self-control, her mind must even then be agonized by the complicated pangs of terror and remorse. For, what imagination can conceive her tremors, lest at every succeeding moment *Macbeth*, in his distraction, may confirm those suspicions, but ill concealed, under the loyal looks and cordial manners of their facile courtiers, when, with smothered terror, yet domineering indignation, she exclaims, upon his agitation at the ghost of *Banquo,* 'Are you a man?' *Macbeth* answers,

'Aye, a bold one—that dare look on that
Which might appal the devil.'

Lady Macbeth.

'Oh, proper stuff!
This is the very painting of your fear;
This is the air-drawn dagger which, ye said,
Led you to Duncan:—Oh, these flaws and starts,
Impostors to true fear, would well become
A woman's story at a winter's fire,

Authorized by her grandam—Shame itself.
Why do you make such faces? when all's done,
You look but on a stool.'

Dying with fear, yet assuming the utmost composure, she returns to her stately canopy; and, with trembling nerves, having tottered up the steps to her throne, that bad eminence, she entertains her wondering guests with frightful smiles, with over-acted attention, and with fitful graciousness; painfully, yet incessantly, labouring to divert their attention from her husband. Whilst writhing thus under her internal agonies, her restless and terrifying glances towards *Macbeth*, in spite of all her efforts to suppress them, have thrown the whole table into amazement; and the murderer then suddenly breaks up the assembly, by the following confession of his horrors:

'Can such things be,
And overcome us like a summer cloud,
Without our special wonder? You make me
Even to the disposition that I am,
When now I think you can behold such sights
And keep the natural ruby of your cheeks,
When mine is blanched with fear.'

Rosse.

'What sight, my lord?'

What imitation, in such circumstances as these, would ever satisfy the demands of expectation? The terror, the remorse, the hypocrisy of this astonishing being, flitting in frightful succession over her countenance, and actuating her agitated gestures with her varying emotions, present, perhaps, one of the greatest difficulties of the scenic art, and cause her representative no less to tremble for the suffrage of her private study, than for its public effect.

It is now the time to inform you of an idea which I have conceived of *Lady Macbeth*'s character, which perhaps will appear as fanciful as that which I have adopted respecting the style of her beauty; and, in order to justify this idea, I must carry you back to the scene immediately preceding the banquet, in which you will recollect the following dialogue:

'Oh, full of scorpions is my mind, dear wife;
Thou knowest that Banquo and his Fleance live.'

Lady Macbeth.

'But in them Nature's copy's not eterne.'

Macbeth.

'There's comfort yet—they are assailable.
Then be thou jocund; ere the bat has flown
His cloistered flight—ere to black Hecate's summons
The shard-born beetle with his drowsy hums
Hath rung night's yawning peal—there shall be done

A deed of dreadful note.'

Lady Macbeth.

'What's to be done?'

Macbeth.

'Be innocent of the knowledge, dearest chuck,
Till thou applaud the deed. Come, unfeeling night,
Scarf up the tender, pitiful eye of day,
And with thy bloody and invisible hand
Cancel and tear to pieces that great bond
Which keeps me pale. Light thickens, and the crow
Makes way to the rooky wood.—
Good things of day begin to droop and drowze,
While night's black agents to their prey do rouse.
Thou marvellest at my words—but hold thee still;
Things bad begun, make strong themselves by ill.'

Now, it is not possible that she should hear all these ambiguous hints about *Banquo* without being too well aware that a sudden, lamentable fate awaits him. Yet, so far from offering any opposition to *Macbeth*'s murderous designs, she even hints, I think, at the facility, if not the expediency, of destroying both *Banquo* and his equally unoffending child, when she observes that, *'in them Nature's copy is not eterne.'* Having, therefore, now filled the measure of her crimes, I have imagined that the last appearance of *Banquo's* ghost became no less visible to her eyes than it became to those of her husband. Yes, the spirit of the noble *Banquo* has smilingly filled up, even to overflowing, and now commends to her own lips the ingredients of her poisoned chalice.

"The Fifth Act.

Behold her now, with wasted form, with wan and haggard countenance, her starry eyes glazed with the ever-burning fever of remorse, and on their lids the shadows of death. Her ever-restless spirit wanders in troubled dreams about her dismal apartment; and, whether waking or asleep, the smell of innocent blood incessantly haunts her imagination:

'Here's the smell of the blood still.
All the perfumes of Arabia will not sweeten
This little hand.'

"How beautifully contrasted is this exclamation with the bolder image of *Macbeth*, in expressing the same feeling!

'Will all great Neptune's ocean wash the blood
Clean from this hand?'

And how appropriately either sex illustrates the same idea!

During this appalling scene, which, to my sense, is the

most so of them all, the wretched creature, in imagination, acts over again the accumulated horrors of her whole conduct. These dreadful images, accompanied with the agitations they have induced have obviously accelerated her untimely end: for in a few moments the tidings of her death are brought to her unhappy husband. It is conjectured that she died by her own hand. Too certain it is, that she dies, and makes no sign. I have now to account to you for the weakness which I have, a few lines back, ascribed to *Macbeth*; and I am not quite without hope that the following observations will bear me out in my opinion. Please to observe, that he (I must think pusillanimously, when I compare his conduct to her forbearance,) has been continually pouring out his miseries to his wife. His heart has therefore been eased, from time to time, by unloading its weight of woe; while she, on the contrary, has perseveringly endured in silence the uttermost anguish of a wounded spirit.

'The grief that does not speak
Whispers the o'erfraught heart, and bids it break.'

Her feminine nature, her delicate structure, it is too evident, are soon overwhelmed by the enormous pressure of her crimes. Yet it will be granted, that she gives proofs of a naturally higher toned mind than that of *Macbeth*. The different physical powers of the two sexes are finely delineated, in the different effects which their mutual crimes produce. Her frailer frame, and keener feelings, have now sunk under the struggle—his robust and less sensitive constitution has not only resisted it, but bears him on to deeper wickedness, and to experience the fatal fecundity of crime.

> 'For mine own good—All causes shall give way.
> I am in blood so far stepp'd in, that should I wade
> no more,
> Returning were as tedious as go o'er.'

Henceforth, accordingly, he perpetrates horrors to the day of his doom.

In one point of view, at least, this guilty pair extort from us, in spite of ourselves, a certain respect and approbation. Their grandeur of character sustains them both above recrimination (the despicable accustomed resort of vulgar minds,) in adversity; for the wretched husband, though almost impelled into this gulph of destruction by the instigations of his wife, feels no abatement of his love for her, while she, on her part, appears to have known no tenderness for him, till, with a heart bleeding at every pore, she beholds in him the miserable victim of their mutual ambition. Unlike the first frail pair in Paradise, they spent not the fruitless hours in mutual accusation.

Sarah Siddons' portrayal was to establish a standard for all future interpretations. Throughout her career, she meticulously prepared her roles. After her retirement, she advised the young actor William Macready to "study, study, study."[31]

In the summer of 1774, Mrs. Siddons was seen as Belvidera by Lord Bruce. He was an acquaintance of David Garrick and recommended the actress to the noted actor-manager. Garrick engaged her in 1775 for his final season at Drury Lane. She made her debut on December 29, 1775, as Portia in *The Merchant of Venice*. Unaccustomed to the vastness of this London theatre and paralyzed by stage fright, Mrs. Siddons' voice frequently was inaudible. In addition, her movements were awkward. Next she was cast in several comic parts to which she was ill suited. Her final role of the season was Lady Anne in *Richard III*, and her performance was declared "lamentable."[32] She was not re-engaged and returned to acting in the provinces for the next six years.

Although she had failed in her first London season, Mrs. Siddons had been deeply affected by the realism of Garrick's acting. She strove to perfect her speech and movement. Also she gained needed experience and confidence by performing in an average of 30 different plays a season. And she revealed a talent for both sentimental and heroic tragedy. Her outstanding portrayals were of monumental women motivated by intense emotions. "I do think that Mrs. Siddons," the writer Hester Thrale Piozzi was to record, "for Vigor of Action, pathetic Tone of Voice, and a sort of Radiance which comes round her in Scenes where strong heroic Virtues are displayed, *never had her Equal*."[33] But she was unsuccessful in either romantic or comic roles.

By 1782, she had become the leading actress of the Theatre Royal in Bath, England's foremost provincial company. Richard Brinsley Sheridan the playwright and theatre manager offered her a contracted at Drury Lane.

Mrs. Siddons made her second London debut on October 10, 1782, as Isabella in Southerne's *The Fatal Marriage*. She had matured in artistry since her first performance there in 1775 and now captivated the audience. They were fascinated by the distinct articulation, elegant movements, and classical beauty of the tall, well-proportioned, auburn-haired, dark-eyed, symmetrically-featured actress who showed extraordinary talent for pathos. Overnight Sarah Siddons had become the leading tragedienne of England, an eminence she was to maintain until her retirement in 1812.

She and her brother, the noted actor John Philip Kemble, inaugurated a new style of acting referred to as the "Kemble school" which emphasized grandeur. Mrs. Siddons' imposing size and serious mien undoubtedly fostered her solemn movements, statuesque poses, and formal, elevated speech ideally suited to tragic heroines of her repertoire. Her versatile voice and large mobile features were capable of rapid emotional transitions from melting tenderness to thundering fury. Contemporary accounts recorded that the flash of her eyes was visible at the rear of the auditorium. Her whispered phrases carried to the topmost galleries. She was also expert at silent pantomime. Macready wrote of her performance as Mrs. Beverley in the debtor's prison scene from Edward Moore's *The Gamester*:

> The climax to her sorrows and sufferings was in the dungeon, when on her knees, holding her dying husband, he dropped lifeless from her arms. Her glaring eyes were fixed in stony blankness on Beverley's face; the powers of life seemed suspended in her; her sister and Lewson gently seized her, and slowly led her unresisting from the body, her gaze never for an instant averted from it; when they reached the prison door she stopped, as if awakened from a trance, with a shriek of agony that would have pierced the hardest heart, and rushing from them, flung herself as if for union in death on the prostrate form before her.34

Mrs. Siddons was a theatrical innovator who rejected the traditional stage actions of her predecessors. As Lady Macbeth she refused to carry a candle throughout the sleepwalking scene as had been done by Mrs. Pritchard. She wrote of her first performance in that role at Drury Lane:

> The dreaded first night at length arrived, when, just as I had finished my toilette, and was pondering with fearfulness my first appearance in the grand fiendish part, comes Mr. Sheridan, knocking at my door, and insisting, in spite of all my entreaties not to be interrupted at this to me tremendous moment, to be admitted. He would not be denied admittance; for he protested he must speak to me on a circumstance which so deeply concerned my own interest, that it was of the most serious nature. Well, after much squabbling, I was compelled to admit him, that I might dismiss him the sooner, and compose myself before the play began. But, what was my distress and astonishment, when I found that he wanted me, even at this moment of anxiety and terror, to adopt another mode of acting the sleeping scene. He told me he had heard with the greatest surprise and concern that I meant to act it without holding the candle in my hand; and, when I urged the impracticability of washing out that '*damned spot*,' with the vehemence that was certainly implied by both her own words, and by those of her gentlewoman, he insisted, that if I did put the candle out of my hand, it would be thought a presumptuous innovation, as Mrs. Pritchard has always retained it in hers.

My mind, however, was made up, and it was then too late to make me alter it; for I was too agitated to adopt another method. My deference for Mr. Sheridan's taste and judgment was, however, so great, that, had he proposed the alteration whilst it was possible for me to change my own plan, I should have yielded to his suggestion; though, even then, it would have been against my own opinion, and my observation of the accuracy with which somnambulists perform all the acts of waking persons. The scene, of course, was acted as I had myself conceived it; and the innovation, as Mr. Sheridan called it, was received with approbation. Mr. Sheridan himself came to me, after the play, and most ingenuously congratulated me on my obstinacy. When he was gone out of the room I began to undress; and, while standing up before my glass, and taking off my mantle, a diverting circumstance occurred, to chase away the feelings of this anxious night; for, while I was repeating, and endeavouring to call to mind the appropriate tone and action to the following words, 'Here's the smell of blood still!" my dresser innocently exclaimed, 'Dear me, ma'am, how very hysterical you are to-night; I protest and vow, ma'am, it was not blood, but rose-pink and water; for I saw the property-man mix it up with my own eyes.'35

The actress combined elements of realism with formalized movements and speech.

This same realism was evident in Mrs. Siddons' psychological identification with her roles. Following a performance of Otway's *Venice Preserved*, she claimed: "...it is hardly acting, it seemed to me, and I believe to the audience, almost reality; ...I felt every word as if I were the real person, and not the representative."[36] Unlike many of her colleagues, who frequently acknowledged or even spoke to friends in the audience during a performance, Mrs. Siddons was completely absorbed in her portrayals. She wrote of her performance as Constance in Shakespeare's *King John*:

> Whenever I was called upon to personate the character of *Constance*, I never, from the beginning of the play to the end of my part in it, once suffered my dressing-room door to be closed, in order that my attention might be constantly fixed on those distressing events which, by this means, I could plainly hear going on upon the stage, the terrible effects of which progress were to be represented by me.... In short, the spirit of the whole drama took possession of my mind and frame, by my attention being incessantly riveted to the passing scenes.[37]

Her audiences were transported by the vividness of her portrayals. She did not underplay minor scenes in order to emphasize moments of high emotion but maintained throughout an appropriate level of dramatic intensity. The actress' physical and emotional transitions were an integral part of her character portrayal. George III praised her "total repose in certain situations," in contrast to the acting of David Garrick. "He never could stand still," commented the King, "He was a great fidget."[38]

As of 1794, Mrs. Siddons' style of presentation gradually changed. Accommodations were necessary to suit the increased size of the new Drury Lane theatre which seated 3,600 compared to the former capacity of 2,200. She broadened her gestures and increased her use of declamation.

At the same time, she simplified her costumes and hairstyles, discarding hooped petticoats, head plumes, and large side curls. Instead, she adopted high waisted Directoire gowns covered by gracefully draped shawls and mantles. Her unpowdered hair was knotted behind her head, and she wore as headgear veils, crowns, or turbans.

Mrs. Siddons was popular with England's leading writers and painters. Joshua Reynolds, Thomas Gainsborough, Gilbert Stuart, George Romney, and Thomas Lawrence painted portraits of her. And she was appointed Preceptress in English Reading to the Princesses by George III. Like her artistic progenitor, Mary Saunderson Betterton, Sarah Siddons taught elocution to the royal children.

The actress' private life, however, was unhappy. Her husband managed the household and brought up their seven children. But William Siddons was jealous of his wife's accomplishments and treated her indifferently. He may have given her venereal disease. Sarah Siddons found acting "a vent for her private sorrows."[39]

In 1802, Mrs. Siddons and her brother left Drury Lane because of Sheridan's poor management. Both accepted contracts at Covent Garden, where Mrs. Siddons remained until her retirement from the stage on June 29, 1812. Her final appearance was as Lady Macbeth, and the audience insisted upon the performance's conclusion with her sleepwalking scene.

Five years later, when John Philip Kemble retired from Covent Garden, a public dinner was given in his honor. No such tribute had been accorded to his distinguished sister. "Well," she commented, "perhaps in the next world women will be more valued than they are in this."[40]

For many years Sarah Siddons gave public readings from the works of Milton and Shakespeare. On June 8, 1831, she died at the age of 76. Her interment in the churchyard of St. Mary's in Paddington was attended by 5,000 people. The entire companies from Covent Garden and Drury Lane occupied 11 coaches in the funeral cortege. Eighteen years later, a statue of Mrs. Siddons was placed in Westminster Abbey upon the insistence of William Macready.

Only 122 years had elapsed from the debut of Mrs. Betterton in 1660 to the second London appearance of Mrs. Siddons in 1782. Yet women players had perfected their art and attained professional status, social acceptance, and even respect.

CHAPTER FOUR
AMERICA 1752-1876

Sarah Siddons' younger sister Elizabeth Kemble Whitlock was a successful actress in the English provinces. She was a massive woman with a deep and powerful voice, but lacked both the beauty and elegance of her famous sister. In 1794, she accepted a contract at the Chestnut Street Theatre in Philadelphia and "found across the Atlantic a fortune and celebrity which it would have been difficult for her to have achieved under the disadvantages of proximity to, and comparison with, her sister, Mrs. Siddons."[1] By the end of the eighteenth century, numerous actors and actresses who had not attained stardom in England established successful careers in America.

The first prominent actress in the New World was Mrs. Lewis Hallam, leading lady of an English troupe which landed at Yorktown in June 1752. The company had been assembled by William Hallam, bankrupt proprietor of the minor London theatre New Wells at Goodman's Fields, in the hope of recouping his losses. This was not the first professional theatre company to appear in America. In 1749, Walter Murray and Thomas Kean had formed a troupe in the colonies and for several years had performed in New York, Pennsylvania, Virginia, Maryland, and South Carolina. But the Hallam Company, under the directorship of William's brother Lewis, was the first professional English troupe to visit America.

Lewis Hallam and his wife had been leading players at Goodman's Fields. He generally appeared as low comedian and she as gentle heroine of tragedy and as lively or languid heroine of sentimental or high comedy. Mrs. Hallam's repertoire of over forty roles had included Lady Anne, Lady Percy, Jane Shore, Maria (Lillo's *The London Merchant*), Lady Townley (*The Provoked Husband*), Angelica (*Love for Love*), Miranda (*The Tempest*), Violante (Theobald's *The Double Falsehood*), and Lady Betty Modish (*The Careless Husband*).

After reconstructing Murray and Kean's theatre in Williamsburg, the Hallam Company opened on September 15 with *The Merchant of Venice* featuring Mrs. Hallam as Portia. For the next two and a half years, they remained in America performing seasons in Williamsburg, Annapolis, New York, and Charleston. They wisely avoided Puritan New England. They either built or remodeled theatres in which they presented their repertory of more than 30 plays and farces. All had been thoroughly rehearsed during the six-week voyage on board the *Charming Sally*. Aside from Portia, Mrs. Hallam was seen in roles such as Juliet, Cordelia, Jane Shore, Calista (*The Fair Penitent*), Mrs. Beverley (*The Gamester*), Andromache (*The Distrest Mother*), Lady Betty Modish, Indiana (*The Conscious Lovers*), Angelica, and Mrs. Sullen (*The Beaux' Stratagem*). It is reported that she was "a woman of great beauty and elegance, still in the prime of life, and enabled to play youthful heroines of tragedy and comedy with due effect."[2] And another viewer wrote that "an Epilogue...was presented by Mrs. Hallam, with all the Graces and Gesture, and the Propriety of Elocution, and met with universal and loud applause."[3]

The Hallams had four children -- Lewis Jr., Helen (or Sarah), Adam, and Isabella. Little is known of Helen and Adam. Lewis Hallam Jr. eventually became a leading American actor-manager. Isabella Hallam Mattocks established herself as a popular comedienne for 52 years at London's Covent Garden.

In 1755, the Hallam Company traveled to Jamaica where Lewis

Hallam Sr. died in 1756. Two years later, Mrs. Hallam married David Douglass, an actor with another English troupe which had been in Jamaica since 1751. The two companies were amalgamated under the management of Douglass. Mrs. Hallam-Douglass was the new troupe's leading lady with her son Lewis Jr. as leading man. The company headed for America that same year. Until the Continental Congress closed all theatres in 1774, they performed continuously in New York, Philadelphia, Annapolis, and Charleston.

By 1764, the middle-aged Mrs. Douglass had given up her more youthful roles and appeared as the mature Gertrude (*Hamlet*), Lady Randolph (Home's *Douglas*), and the Duchess of York (*Richard III*). "A respectable, matron-like dame," recalls an early nineteenth-century author, "stately or querulous as occasion required, a very good Gertrude, a truly appropriate Lady Randolph with her white handkerchief and her weeds; but then, to applaud, it was absolutely necessary to forget, that to touch the heart of the spectator had any relation to her function."[4] And the manager and playwright William Dunlap recalled that he often "heard old ladies speak, almost in raptures, of the beauty and grace of Mrs. Douglass, and the pathos of her personation of Jane Shore."[5] Nothing is really known of her acting style, but her son Lewis was noted for his stiff poses and formal declamation or rant.

Mrs. Douglass died in a tavern near Philadelphia's Southwark Theatre in 1774. Her death may have been the aftereffect of an injury sustained in the theatre. Apparently she was highly regarded because it is reported that "all the ladies in the neighborhood attended her funeral"[6] at the Second Presbyterian Church on Arch and Third Streets. The graveyard in which she lay buried was later destroyed.

Although there were other English actresses who followed Mrs. Douglass, none compared to Ann Brunton Merry. Ann Brunton was born on May 30, 1769, in London. Her father John Brunton was a tea dealer. Later he became an actor and then manager of the Theatre Royal Norwich. Ann was educated by her parents and learned to read Shakespeare. Her theatrical career began by accident. According to William Dunlap, John Brunton "coming home from rehearsal one day... overheard her reciting Calista's speech upon the unfortunate condition of her sex, and, on expressing his surprise at the talents she displayed, he found that she had studied and could recite the parts of Juliet, Belvidera and Euphrasia."[7]

John Brunton arranged for his daughter's debut at Bath on February 17, 1785, as Euphrasia (Murphy's *The Grecian Daughter*). This was followed with performances of the youthful Horatia (Whitehead's *The Roman Father*) and Palmira (Voltaire's *Mahomet*). The fifteen-year-old actress was offered a contract at Covent Garden, where she appeared first as Horatia on October 17, 1785. Ann Brunton was an instant success and for the next seven years performed the roles of Juliet, Monimia (*The Orphan*), Hermione (*The Distrest Mother*), Alicia (*Jane Shore*), and Cordelia. In addition, she played the romantic roles of Indiana (*The Conscious Lovers*), Perdita (*The Winter's Tale*), and Beatrice (*Much Ado About Nothing*). She was acclaimed "another Siddons," but their acting styles differed radically. "Mrs. Siddons had person, power, art, beyond all contemporaries," wrote Dunlap, " -- [Ann Brunton] had voice and feeling, that went as direct to the heart of a feeling auditor as the ray of light to its destination. -- Their persons and manners were indeed opposite, and, as we have said above, though [Ann Brunton] made her way direct to the heart, the prize was won by gentleness. But Siddons seized upon it with a force that was irresistible."[8] Sarah Siddons was tall and regal, while Ann Brunton was "rather under size, but her figure was elegant, and her action and deportment graceful and easy."[9] Unlike Mrs. Siddons, Ann Brunton was not strikingly beautiful, but she had equally "expressive features."[10] Both actresses were noted for their superb voices and distinct articulation. Siddons' voice was marked by grandeur of tone and formality of speech. Brunton's "sweetness of voice struck every ear like a charm. Entirely devoid of stage rant, she read with perfect ease and freedom, laying her accent and emphasis naturally and with critical correctness."[11]

In 1791, Ann Brunton married the poet and gambler Robert Merry. Her husband insisted that she retire from the stage in 1792. By 1796, however, Merry was financially ruined and encouraged his wife to sign a contract with the Chestnut Street Theatre Company in Philadelphia. She made her debut on December 5, 1796, as Juliet and once again was an instant success. Following her 1797 appearance in New York, Ann Merry was acknowledged as America's foremost tragedienne.

In addition to Juliet, she performed Calista (*The Fair Penitent*), Belvidera (*Venice Preserved*), Monimia (*The Orphan*), Euphrasia, Jane Shore, and Ophelia. "Mrs. Merry's Calista...was perfect," wrote a reviewer,

> ...all we can do is to pay a tribute to her generally as an actress....No one perhaps has a more perfect delivery, she seems to give every word its due emphasis, and every syllable its proper accent...pauses are admirable, particularly her emphatic ones, and those too which make the divisions of sense, this last is never interrupted by a mismanagement of breath. In her tones or the modulation of her voice she is equally unexceptionable, varying the sound to the sentiment she gives it that peculiar force and grace which the author designed.[12]

Of her Juliet, the *New York Evening Post* wrote:

> On her entrance loud and reiterated welcome was heard from every part of the house. This tumultuous expression of their delight gave place, at the first word she uttered, to the more characteristic manner of our audience. -- HUSH! SHE SPEAKS! seemed to be the common sensation...when the tragedian can excite that expressive silence, which last evening was produced by the MAGIC SWEETNESS OF JULIET's voice, it is the most unequivocal mark of admiration and respect an audience can bestow, or a performer receive.[13]

Wisely, Ann Merry refused the highly dramatic role of Lady Macbeth. She believed her portrayal would not equal that of Mrs. Siddons, whose performance she had seen in London. Melting sweetness rather than emotional power was her forte.

Ann Merry was a brilliant theatrical technician and aware of her own histrionic strengths. She performed only those roles which suited her specific talents. Dunlap referred to her as "the most perfect actress America has seen"[14] and "perhaps the best representative of Juliet that was ever seen or heard."[15]

Merry became a widow in 1798. On January 1, 1803, she married Thomas Wignell the American theatre manager who had brought her to Philadelphia. Wignell died seven weeks later and left her co-owner with Alexander Reinagle of the Chestnut Street Theatre. The actress gave birth to a daughter after her husband's death and in 1806 married the actor William Warren. On June 28, 1808, she died in Gadsby's Tavern,

Alexandria, Virginia, after giving birth to a stillborn son. They were buried together in Alexandria's Episcopalian cemetery.

Two years after Ann Warren's death, the 16-year-old English dancer and actress Mary Ann Dyke Duff landed in Boston. She was soon to be recognized as her predecessor's equal "in pathos."[16] Mary Ann Dyke was born in 1794 in London. She was the eldest daughter of an East India Company employee. Following her father's death abroad, she began to study dancing for a theatrical career and was a student of James D'eqville, ballet master of the King's Theatre. She made her debut in 1807 at the Dublin Theatre. In 1810, she married the talented young Irish actor John R. Duff, who had signed a contract at Boston's Federal Street Theatre.

Duff soon became a popular actor in Boston, Philadelphia, and Baltimore. But despite his wife's melodic voice, radiant dark eyes, tall, perfectly proportioned frame and simple manner, her histrionic "style" was referred to as "indifferent."[17] "She lacked both conception and power," wrote a Boston critic of her Juliet. The Philadelphia and Baltimore theatre manager William B. Wood termed her "tame and indolent."[18] She was considered best in pantomime and ballet.

By 1818, however, a major change was noted in Mrs. Duff's acting. Her husband's career had faded, and he was often ill with gout. The couple now had children to support. "It has been surmised," wrote Joseph N. Ireland, the nineteenth-century American theatre historian and biographer, "that anxiety for her family was the chief cause of Mrs. Duff's awakened energy and desire to excell in a profession, which in earlier life she had felt unnecessary and had been indifferent to."[19] In Boston, the actress' Juliet "had all the loveliness and innocence of youth, the fervor and force of passion, the ecstacy of joy, and the agony of grief, terror, and despair, combined in her most harmonious and powerfully developed personation."[20] She also appeared as Desdemona, Ophelia, and Jane

Shore. But her greatest success was as Hermione in *The Distrest Mother*. "The Bostonians first fully appreciated her genius and talents," stated Ireland, "and, in which, throwing aside all tameness and restraint, she perhaps first fully developed the fire and passion that had long been slumbering in her soul."[21]

In February 1821, Duff repeated this role in a performance starring the distinguished English actor Edmund Kean as Orestes. It is reported that "while rehearsing...Mr. Kean is said to have requested her to play with less force and intensity, or her acting would throw him into the background; to which she replied that, though she honored his rank and position in the profession, her duty to herself and the public would constrain her always to play to the best of her ability."[22] Both artists shared the evening's success. In addition, she performed Ophelia to Kean's Hamlet, Cordelia to his King Lear, and Belvidera to the actor's Jaffeir (*Venice Preserved*). Kean claimed that Mrs. Duff was "the superior of any actress on the British stage."[23] The following year, she performed Cordelia and Ophelia to the Lear and Hamlet of another popular English actor Junius Brutus Booth. He pronounced her "the greatest actress in the world."[24] Her successes continued in Philadelphia and Baltimore.

On September 5, 1823, Duff made her debut at New York's Park Street Theatre in the role of Hermione to the Orestes of Booth. She then performed Calanthe (*Damon and Pythias*), Lady Macbeth, Tullia (Payne's *Brutus*), Roxana (Lee's *Alexander the Great*), Imogine (Simms' *Bertram*), and Mrs. Beverley (*The Gamester*). The press lauded her acting, but society ignored her performances. "New York dilettanti seemed to consider it a piece of presumption," surmised Ireland, "for a stock actress from the Boston and Philadelphia theatres to present herself as a star on the Metropolitan stage, and many of them in consequence avoided the theatre during her stay."[25] Never again did the actress appear at the Park

Street Theatre. Instead, her future New York performances were at the less prestigious Bowery, Richmond Hill Chatham Garden, and Franklin Theatres. She remained popular with the press and developed an enthusiastic public. The noted American journalist Horace Greeley recalled: "I saw Mrs. Duff personate Lady Macbeth better than it has since been done in this city....I doubt that any woman has since played in our city...who was the superior to Mrs. Duff in a wide range of tragic characters."[26] New York society, however, remained aloof unlike the Brahmin ladies of Boston who adopted the actress' "perfect diction, propriety of action and simple dignity of manner...as standards of excellence worthy of their closest study."[27]

Some of Mary Ann Duff's finest portrayals were Queen Katherine, Lady Macbeth, Belvidera, Mrs. Haller (Kotzebue's *The Stranger*), Hermione, Mathilde (*The Bohemian Mother*), Cordelia, Ophelia, Lady Randolph (*Douglas*), and Jane Shore. She was referred to as "the American Siddons." Like the English tragedienne, Mary Ann Duff excelled in the representation of intense emotions and was noted for her regal dignity. She also was of a serious nature and maintained an intense psychological identification with her characters. According to a New York critic:

> Mrs. Duff has one great characteristic...and that is UNIFORMITY OF EXCELLENCE. She makes no points. We cannot say of her as we used to say of Kean, - 'that's a beautiful touch.'...From beginning to end, from her first entrance to her final exit you see before you only the character she is personating. The unity of her conception - the ONENESS - is remarkable. No temptation can induce her to break it....She seems to have a separate existence

during the continuance of the play and to have lost all knowledge of, and even all power of seeing, the realities around her,...In every line, in every word, she is true to the author, and departs not in a single instance from her delineation."[28]

By 1828, the Duffs journeyed to England with the hope of attaining international renown. After performances in Brighton, she made her debut as Isabella (Southerne's *Isabella*) at Drury Lane on March 3, 1828. Her acting was hampered by severe stage fright. The ensuing reviews were mixed. Living in London was expensive for the Duffs and their numerous children. The actress and her family soon returned to America, where she resumed her successful engagements in Boston, Philadelphia, and New York.

On April 28, 1831, John Duff died, leaving his wife the sole supporter of their ten children. Until this time, she had been America's unrivaled queen of tragedy. However, in 1832, the glamorous and talented young English tragedienne Fanny Kemble arrived in New York. Thirty-eight-year-old Mary Ann Duff realized that she could not compete with the twenty-two-year-old London star. She embarked on an acting tour of the western and southern states. While traveling on a Mississippi steamer, she selflessly tended cholera victims.

By 1833, Mary Ann Duff was deeply in debt. She married the actor Charles Young, who had promised to bestow a recent inheritance on her children. When the actress learned that her husband was penniless, she left him. The marriage was annulled, and Duff suffered a nervous breakdown. For six months she was unable to act, but by January 1834, she was performing again in Philadelphia and Baltimore.

In 1836, she married a lawyer Joel G. Seaver and retired from the stage. During her nearly 30 years in the theatre, Duff performed more than 220 roles. Several were in works by American playwrights such as Deela in Mordecai M. Noah's *She Would be a Soldier, or the Battle of Chippewa*, Mary in James N. Barker's *Superstition*, and the Indian Nahmeokee in John A. Stone's *Metamora*. So indelible was the impression made by this performer that many years after her retirement, the noted actor John Gilbert recalled: "She was, without exception, the most exquisite tragic actress he ever saw."[29]

The couple settled in New Orleans. Mary Ann Seaver was converted to Methodism and for the next 18 years devoted herself to charitable works. But apparently by 1854, the Seavers' marriage was overcast by "the shadow of a heavy cloud."[30] Joel Seaver moved to Texas, and his wife went to live with her daughter, Matilda I. Reillieux, in New York. On September 5, 1857, the former actress died of cancer. She was buried in Brooklyn's Greenwood Cemetery.

When Mary Ann Duff retired from the theatre in 1836, the young actress Charlotte Cushman made her debut as Lady Macbeth on April 23 in New Orleans. She was to become America's first internationally acclaimed tragedienne. Cushman was a New England blue blood. Her ancestor Robert Cushman was financial agent for the Pilgrim Fathers, and his son Thomas was ruling elder at Plymouth's First Church from 1649 to 1692. One hundred and twenty-four years later, Charlotte Saunders Cushman was born in Boston on July 23, 1816.

Cushman was an energetic child, exploring the busy wharves and dominating the games of her playmates. After Charlotte Cushman had been taken to see the noted English actor William Macready as Coriolanus, she and her friends performed plays and operettas in the family attic. Cushman always assumed the lead. She was an excellent mimic, delighting her sister Susan and brothers Charlie and Augustus with imitations ranging from the cackling of a hen to the mannerisms of the local Unitarian minister.

Since her uncle August Babbitt was a stockholder of the new Tremont Theatre, Cushman was allowed to attend performances. She saw the English stars Thomas A. Cooper and Mrs. Powell. Both were exponents of the Kemble school, emphasizing grandeur of manner, statuesque poses, and formal, elevated speech.

Her artistic inclinations were aroused, and she soon revealed a marked ability at reading aloud. Charlotte Cushman recalled:

> I remember on one occasion reading a scene from Howard Payne's tragedy of 'Brutus,' in which Brutus speaks, and the immediate result was my elevation to the head of the class, to the evident disgust of my competitors, who grumbled out, 'No wonder she can read, she goes to the theatre.' I had been before this very shy and reserved, not to say stupid, about reading in school, afraid of the sound of my own voice, and very unwilling to trust it; but the greater familiarity with the theatre seemed suddenly to unloose my tongue, and give birth as it were to a faculty which has been the ruling passion ever since.[31]

Cushman was not only an excellent reader, but also fine singer and capable pianist. Her voice was developing into a full contralto with a secure upper register, and she began to consider singing as a career. By 1829, however, her father's business had failed and no funds were available for lessons. She left school and assisted her mother in running a boarding house. But in 1832, William Paddon Boston's leading vocal pedagogue consented to give her lessons in exchange for domestic services. She studied with him for nine months.

The following year, she auditioned for the noted English singers Joseph and Mary Ann Wood. They encouraged this intensely serious young woman's vocal aspirations. She even was asked to perform duets with Mrs. Wood during two of her Boston concerts. When the Woods' accompanist and coach James G. Maeder remained in Boston as the Tremont Theatre's musical director, Cushman studied singing with him.

On April 8, 1835, she made her operatic debut at the Tremont Theatre in the soprano role of Countess Almaviva in Mozart's *The Marriage of Figaro*. The press agreed on her future potential. Maeder obtained a season's contract for the 19-year-old singer at the St. Charles Theatre in New Orleans. Again she was to perform the Countess, but by now the strain of singing a role completely out of her vocal range was evident in her strident upper register. The press was scathing in its denunciation of her singing.

After receiving equally disastrous reviews in other roles, Cushman was advised by the theatre's director James H. Caldwell to consider acting rather than singing as a career. He suggested that she "study some parts"[32] with James Barton, the company's English tragedian, who was an advocate of the Kemble school. Barton was a studious actor. He taught her the traditional English stage business and line readings for her roles.

When they began to study Lady Macbeth, the self-conscious young actress was unable to release her emotions. Barton finally resorted to subterfuge. "I put her into a towering rage," he recalled, "by certain rude remarks I purposely made, and then at last there blazed forth the fire and passion I knew were smouldering within."[33] Also revealed was a deep, powerful, interestingly husky speaking voice with a wide range because of her vocal training.

The tall, broad-shouldered performer with her square jaw, firm mouth, and penetrating gray-blue eyes began to infuse the role with her own vigorous personality. "She was incarnate power," William Winter was to write of her in later years. "She dominated by intrinsic authority;" he wrote, "she was a woman born to command."[34] Her Lady Macbeth was a pantherine, imperious, often inebriated woman driven by mad ambition. She ruled her husband, compelling him to murder King Duncan and to grasp the crown of Scotland. "She bullies Macbeth;" recorded her colleague George Vandenhoff, "gets him into a corner of the stage, and... as I heard a man with more force than elegance, express it...she 'pitches into him;' in fact, as one sees her large clenched hand and muscular arm threatening him, in alarming proximity, one feels that if other arguments fail with her husband, she will have recourse to blows."[35] When the short and slender Edwin Booth performed Macbeth with her in 1860, he barely could resist exclaiming: "Well, why don't you kill him? You're a great deal bigger than I am."[36] The robust Cushman disagreed with Booth's more subtle acting style, informing him: "Exceedingly interesting, but, dear boy, don't be afraid of overdoing it. Remember Macbeth was the great-grandfather of all the Bowery ruffians."[36]

This same intensity was evident in the sleepwalking scene. "With staring eyes," reported a critic, "fixed and stony, a countenance wrung by the agonies of conscience, and with faltering steps, the actress was magnificently intense and vivid. Her breath came and went in gasps, and long sighs struggled from the heart as if they would tear life from its frail tenement. Her clinging hands, convulsively rubbing at the spot that would not out, were instinct with guilty terror."[37]

Following her successful debut, Charlotte Cushman spent the next eight years performing the roles of Lady Macbeth, Goneril (*King Lear*), Cordelia, Gertrude, Ophelia, Belvidera (*Venice Preserved*), and Mrs. Haller (*The Stranger*) in Albany, Buffalo, Detroit, Boston, Philadelphia, and New York. In 1843, she appeared with William Macready, who encouraged the young American actress to make her debut in London. On February 14, 1845, she opened at the Princess' Theatre in the role of Bianca (Milman's *Fazio*). The press declared her an artistic genius, and she won further acclaim for her Queen Katherine and Romeo to the Juliet of her sister Susan. Queen Victoria requested a command performance of *Henry VIII*. London society and literati opened their doors to this American theatrical star and New England aristocrat.

In 1849, Charlotte Cushman returned to the United States and for 26 years was lionized by the American public. Her portrayals were hallmarked by emotional intensity and energetic action. She was ideally suited to represent women of monolithic stature and temperament. According to a contemporary account: "Her true forte [was] the character of a woman where most of the softer traits of womanhood are wanting, ...or in characters where, roused by passion or incited by some earnest and long cherished determination, the woman for the time being, assumes the power and energy of manhood."[38] This may explain her success in the male roles of Romeo and Claude Melnotte (Bulwer-Lytton's *The Lady of Lyons*).

In addition to Lady Macbeth, Charlotte Cushman's finest portrayals were her commanding, regal Queen Katherine (*Henry VIII*), her frightening, unearthly, ancient gypsy hag Meg Merrilies (Scott's *Guy Mannering*), and her depraved Nancy Sykes (Dickens' *Oliver Twist*). "Her greatest part," recalled George Vandenhoff, "fearfully natural, dreadfully intense, horribly real, was Nancy Sykes...it was too true, it was painful."[39] "She dragged herself onto the stage," recalled the actor Lawrence Barrett of Cushman's dying Nancy, "in a wonderful manner, and, keeping her face away from her audience, produced a feeling of chilly horror by the management of her voice as she called for Bill and begged him to kiss her...it sounded as if she spoke through blood."[40] And according to the American actress Mary Anderson, the death scene of Cushman's Meg Merrilies was equally superlative. "When [the] fatal bullet entered her body," she wrote, "she came staggering down the stage, her terrible shriek,...wild and piercing,...full of agony and yet of the triumph she had given her life to gain."[41]

To those who criticized her restless, incessant movement, the visually unalluring artist replied: "...Siddons was so beautiful of feature that she could well be content to stand still and be gazed at." But of herself she said: "[I] must occupy the eye with action and movement, for if [I] were still [my] beauty would suffer from criticism and half [my] influence be lost."[42] Charlotte Cushman's dramatic talent enabled her to transcend a homely appearance.

A major contribution to her achievement as an actress was complete dedication to her art. At the gala ceremony following her farewell performance in New York as Lady Macbeth on November 7, 1874, she said:

> I was, by press of circumstances, thrown at an early age into a profession for which I had received no special education or training; but I had already, though so young, been brought face to face with necessity. I found life sadly real and intensely earnest, and in my ignorance of other ways of study, I resolved to take therefrom my text and my watchword. To be thoroughly in earnest, intensely in earnest in all my thoughts and in all my actions, whether in my profession or out of it, became my one single idea. And I honestly believe herein lies the secret of my success in life. I do not believe that any great success in any art can be achieved without it.

> I say this to the beginners in my profession, and I am sure all the associates in my art, who have honored me with their presence on this occasion, will endorse what I say in this. Art is an absolute mistress; she will not be coquetted with or slighted; she requires the most entire self-devotion, and she repays with grand triumphs.[43]

According to Lawrence Barrett, she methodically prepared each role "laboriously seeking in every character she played the nicer shades of meaning, the fugitive impressions which elude the superficial scholar; ...tracing in every line for purpose and plan."[44] She advised the young actor James O'Neill to "work, work, work."[45] He later said of her portrayals that "she got more out of the language than anyone I have ever listened to."[47] Her technique for learning lines was described by her friend Emma Stebbins: "A speech would be read...aloud to her, quite slowly and distinctly; then she would repeat what she could of it. Then another reading and another repetition. The third time was generally enough. Then the next speech would be taken up in the same way, and so on."[47] She had a remarkable memory and rarely needed to review the text of a former role. Her diction was immaculate - "not a syllable was lost."[48]

The theatre was Charlotte Cushman's life. She said:

> I think I live and reverence all arts equally, only putting my own just above the others; because in it I recognize the union and culmination of my own. To me it seems as if when God conceived the world, that was Poetry; He formed it, and that was Sculpture; He colored it, and that was Painting; He peopled it with living beings, and that was the grand,

divine, eternal Drama.49

Cushman realized her own worth and demanded the social and financial recognition due a distinguished artist. On one occasion, while talking with the actor John McCullough and the critic William Winter, she "suddenly seized (Winter's) arm with her left hand, and, pointing upward with her right,...said, earnestly and simply, to McCullough: 'I like William Winter, because he puts me up - where I belong.'"50 But it was the naming of a Boston public girls' school in her honor in 1871 that gave Charlotte Cushman the most satisfaction. The actress wrote:

> The City Council paid me a great honor in formally announcing to the world that one of their chief boasts, their public school system, should be associated with my name, by enacting that henceforth and forever the school building which has been erected on the site wherestood the house in which I was born was to be known as the Cushman School. This from old Puritan stock, which believes that the public school is the throne of the state, was a greater honor than any I could have received from them. I was proud, first, that I as an actress had won it; then, secondly, that for the first time this had been bestowed upon a woman; and then came the civic pride, in knowing that my townspeople should care that I was ever born. Nothing in all my life has so pleased me as this.51

Her final stage performance was as Lady Macbeth on May 15, 1875, in Boston. Nine months later, on February 18, 1876, Charlotte Saunders Cushman died of pneumonia in her suite at the Parker House. America's foremost tragedienne left an estate of $500,000 and was buried in Cambridge's Mount Auburn Cemetery amongst Boston's Brahmins and intellectual giants. When William Winter visited the grave site long after her burial, a cemetery workman respectfully exclaimed: "She was considerable of a woman, for a play-actress."[52] Such was her renown.

CHAPTER FIVE
RACHEL 1821-1858

While in London, Charlotte Cushman observed the acting of France's leading tragedienne Rachel and wrote: "I used to look on in perfect rapture of wonder and admiration at her unapproachable art, and often, as I left the theater, and compared my own acting with hers, despair took possession of me, and a mad impulse to end life and effort together."[1]

On February 28, 1821, the wife of an itinerant Jewish peddler from Metz, Germany, gave birth to a daughter at the Golden Sun Inn in Mumpf, Switzerland. Jacob and Esther Félix named their second child Elisa (Elisabeth) Rachel. She was to become the foremost tragedienne of her day and the theatre's first internationally recognized actress.

The Félix family walked throughout Germany, Switzerland, and France selling second-hand clothes from a pushcart. Elisa Félix and her sister Sarah earned money by singing bawdy songs in the streets. Although the actress later was to explain that she recited rather than sang her selections. "Recite is the word," she wrote, "for I have always lacked a soprano voice."[2] By the late 1820's, the Félix family had settled in Lyons, and the girls began to sing in cafes.

In 1830, the Félixs moved to Paris. Elisa Félix and her sister continued to perform and in 1832 were heard by Étienne Choron, director of a school for religious music. They became his students. Choron soon discovered, however, that Elisa Félix's talent was declamation rather than song. He arranged for her to enter the actor Pagnon Saint-Aulaire's school of dramatic art. Saint Aulaire had performed at the Comédie Française and taught Mlle. Félix roles from the plays of Corneille, Racine, and Molière. Apparently, they "were imprinted by him in his pupil's memory, word by word, line by line, intonation by intonation."[3] The young performer studied her parts at home with a copy of the play resting on her knees while she peeled vegetables for the family's meals.

Saint Aulaire's students performed in the Salle Molière, and Elisa Félix was seen in more than thirty roles. Sometimes her voice sounded hoarse, but her diction was precise and energetic. In addition, she possessed nobility of bearing. The French actor and teacher Joseph Isidore Samson saw her perform and later recalled:

> I went to hear her one day, when she was acting in Corneille's *Don Sancho*. I confess that she surprised me by her performance of Isabella, Queen of Castile. I was struck by the tragic pathos she displayed. The divine spark animated this young and fragile creature. She was then so small that she was obliged to raise her head to speak to the actors on the stage with her; yet by her air of queenly dignity she gave you the impression of looking down on them,...The role was imperfectly understood here and there, but she had caught the sentiment and tragedy, and one could foresee the great future in store for this marvelous child.[4]

This same dignity was noted in her manner off stage, and she was most particular about her appearance.

In 1836, she was recommended to Jouslin de la Salle, director of the Comédie Française and was accepted at the Conservatoire. She was to have studied with Samson and Provost, but she soon left the school after being offered only minor roles in student productions. Saint-Aulaire arranged an audition for her with Delestre-Poirson, director of the Theatre du Gymnase, who offered the young actress a contract with his company. She made her debut on April 4, 1837, as the peasant girl Josephine in Paul Duport's melodrama *La Vendéenne* based on Sir Walter Scott's novel *The Heart of Midlothian*. She assumed for the stage her second name: Rachel. Jules Janin, Paris' leading drama critic, wrote of her performance:

> Mademoiselle Rachel acts with much feeling, enthusiasm, and intelligence, but with very little skill. She intuitively understands the part given to her...There is no effort, no exaggeration, no cries, no strained attitudes, and above all no coquetry; on the contrary, she is extremely quiet and dignified, and makes no attempt to move or propitiate her audience by airs and graces...there is a great future in store for this young genius.[5]

Equally impressed by her talent, the famous American actor Edwin Forrest said: "That little bag of bones, with the marble face and the flaming eyes, there is demonical power in her. If she lives, and does not burn out too soon, she will be wonderful."[6]

Rachel did not remain at the Gymnase. The dignity and restraint of her acting were more appropriate to classical tragedy than to melodrama or to comedy. "I am a daughter of the Antique"[7] she later told the playwright François Ponsard, when refusing to perform in his drama *Charlotte Corday*. Her request for an interview at the Comédie Française was ignored. The actress returned to Samson for instruction and also studied history and grammar with his children's governess.

Samson had been a student of the distinguished tragic actor François Joseph Talma, who had renounced the eighteenth century's chant-like declamation in favor of more natural verse speaking. In this respect, he resembled his predecessor, Adrienne Lecouvreur. Talma's style of acting was realistic, and his characterizations were psychologically motivated.

Rachel and Samson spent hours perfecting each intonation and gesture. "Nothing was slurred over," recalled Samson, "nothing was left unstudied. We took note together of every line, of every point to be made."[8] In later years, Rachel was to devote three days practicing the phrase "Ah! Maurice!" from the fifth act of Scribe's *Adrienne Lecouvreur*. "It rings false," she had complained in a rehearsal. "It rings false because you don't know how to say it,"[9] replied Scribe the playwright. Like Talma, she strove for vocal realism. The theatre critic Théophile Gauthier was to write: "Mlle. Rachel's kind of diction, clear, clipped, impassioned, is exactly opposed to the ample periods, the elegant circumlocutions and well-draped phrases of classical poetry."[10]

To develop the appropriate carriage and gestures for her classical heroines of antiquity, Rachel studied Greek and Roman statuary in the Louvre. In addition, she identified herself mentally and emotionally with her roles. After numerous performances of Camille in Corneille's *Horace*, she added new action to the scene in which the young Roman aristocrat learns of her lover's death. Recalling that she had swooned at the description of an accidental amputation, Rachel concluded that Camille's reaction to the dreadful news would be even greater cause for fainting. "During the whole scene," wrote a critic, " the parsimonious author has given his heroine but a single 'helas.' Rachel introduced her by-play, allowing a trembling to cover over her, which increased as the story progressed, when the power over her hands was exhausted, and at the 'helas' she sank motionless into her chair, having vainly endeavored to grasp the arms."[11] Many years later, she was to tell her sister: "In studying for the stage, take my word for it, declamation and gesture are of little avail. You have to think, and to weep."[12]

In 1838, through Samson's influence, Rachel became a member of the Comédie Française. She made her debut as Camille on June 12 to an almost empty house. The small, slender, dark-haired young actress was almost unknown, and society as well as the leading drama critics were away from Paris for the summer. In addition, classical French drama was no longer in favor with the Parisian theatre public. The Romantic movement with Victor Hugo's melodramatic plays had caught the popular fancy. Rachel's debut, however, was attended by Mlle. Mars, the Comédie Française's leading tragedienne, who commented: "She walks the stage well....And she listens well....she does not declaim, she speaks!"[13]

During the next two months, Rachel performed the roles of Emilie (*Cinna*), Hermione (Racine's *Andromaque*), and Amenaide (Voltaire's *Tancrède*). Attendance remained sparse until Jules Janin returned to Paris in September. The critic wrote of Rachel's acting:

> Let me tell you there exists at this moment, at the Theatre Français, an unexpected victory, one of those triumphs of which a nation such as ours has reason to be proud. Those works of art, lost for so long, are at length given back to us. We possess the most marvelous actress (although only still a child) that this generation has seen on the stage. This actress is Mademoiselle Rachel. About a year ago she first appeared at the Gymnase, and I maintained then that she possessed talent of no common order, and that a great future lay before her. I was not believed: people said I exaggerated, and I alone was not strong enough to support

that little girl on that stage. A few days after her first appearance the actress disappeared from the Gymnase, and I, perhaps, was the only person who remembered her, when suddenly she reappears at the Theatre Français in the great tragedies of Corneille, Racine, and Voltaire. Now she is listened to, encouraged, applauded. She has found the legitimate development of her precocious dramatic genius. It is nothing short of marvellous, this uneducated child, without art, without preparation of any kind, thus becoming the interpreter of our grand old tragedies! She blows their ashes into a flame by her genius and her energy.

Do not ask her who Tancrède, Horace, Hermione are, or about the Trojan war, or Pyrrhus, or Helen. She knows nothing; but she has that which is better than knowledge. She has that sudden illumination, which she throws around her; she grows ten inches taller on the stage; she raises her head and extends her chest; her eye brightens; she treads like a sovereign; her voice vibrates instinct with the passion that agitates her. Nothing grander can be conceived than this Camille. To my dying day I will hear that voice and see those tears. She is a priestess, a pythoness, this child of seventeen. The imprecation is the first revelation of Rachel's power. The storm raging in this grief-stricken breast is terrific. We tremble before it as before something superhuman--godlike.[14]

By early October, Rachel was playing to sold-out houses. Even King Louis Philippe, who had not attended the theatre for three years, brought the royal family to see her act. Within a few months, receipts averaged more than 6,000 francs a performance. The actress' salary was raised from 4,000 francs a year to 20,000.

Lacking a formal education, Rachel knew "nothing" about the characters or the legendary background of the dramas in which she performed. But she began to remedy this deficiency. Her artistic success had paved the way to social acceptance. Royalty, society, and literati sought her out. Adolphe Crémieux, future Minister of Justice, taught her the art of letter writing. He even wrote important ones for her . When Rachel admitted to only a familiarity with her own lines, the lawyer explained the plays to her. This was in addition to Samson's character analyses and "short historical lectures."[15] She obviously heeded their instruction because many years later, while preparing for her role in Scribe's *La Czarina*, she wrote: "After dinner...I took down my Biographie Universelle, and looked up Catharine, Empress of Russia, to acquaint myself with a character whom soon I shall have to play. When M. Scribe talks to me about her, I shall know almost as much as he does."[16] In addition, the Marquis de Custine recommended books for her to read. She was befriended by the Duc and Duchesse de Noailles, Madame Récamier, and Chateaubriand. The youthful artist became known for her tact, quiet modesty, dignified elegant manner, wit, and abundant charm. Rachel wore her beautiful but simple clothes "with such art that thinness became a quality."[17] In a letter to her brother Raphaël, she astutely analyzed the reasons for her success in society:

> A woman may attain an honorable position and be esteemed and respected, without possibly having that polish which the world rightly calls 'education.' 'Why?' you may ask. Because by maintaining a great reserve in her language and

demeanor a woman does not lose charm; quite the reverse. A woman answers questions, she does not ask them; she never initiates a discussion; she listens. Retaining what she learns, she acquires without any solid foundation that superficial culture which often passes for the genuine article.[18]

But among her intimates, Rachel often reverted to the vulgar speech and manners of her childhood in the streets and cafes. The tired actress declared that she was in need of being naughty.[19] Like Nell Gwyn, Rachel never attempted to conceal her humble origin. Thus she endeared herself to the middle class. Until the time of her death, they flocked to her performances.

By November 1838, she had added Racine's Eryphile (*Iphigénie en Aulide*) and Monime (*Mithridate*) to her repertoire. All of her portrayals had been successes. But on November 23, her performance of the passionate and vengeful Turkish sultana Roxane (Racine's *Bajazet*) was a total failure. She was overcome by stage fright. For the remainder of her career, she would be hampered by this affliction whenever debuting in a new role. " I am paralyzed;" she admitted, "I feel as if I had chains on."[20] Her second performance, however, was a resounding success. The audience was enthralled by her demoniacal portrayal of a woman driven to murder by frustrated love. In scenes from *Horace* and *Iphigénie*, Rachel had indicated her ability to express scorn, hate, and anger but not with the physical and vocal ferocity revealed as the diabolical, lust-crazed Roxane. Paris had a new queen of tragedy.

Soon the actress' reputation became known abroad. In 1841, she agreed to perform for a month at Her Majesty's Theatre in London . Rachel made her debut on May 10 as Hermione in Racine's *Andromaque* and scored a stunning triumph. According to *The Times*, Rachel demonstrated "complete intelligence of the force of every line....Altogether a more rare combination of intelligence and power has seldom been seen...and when it is recollected that in youth she was almost uneducated, and that her conception of tragic character was originally owing to her own genius, she may be considered almost as a psychological phenomenon."[21] And the noted English actress Fanny Kemble wrote:

> I was immensely struck and carried away with her performance of 'Hermione,'...That in which she is unrivalled by any actor or actress I ever saw is the expression of a certain combined and concentrated hatred and scorn. Her reply to Andromache's appeal to her...was one of the most perfect things I have ever seen on the stage: the cold, cruel, acrid enjoyment of her rival's humiliation, - the quiet, bitter, unmerciful exercise of the power of torture, was certainly, in its keen incisiveness, quite incomparable.[22]

She was equally acclaimed in the roles of Marie Stuart (Lebrun), Emilie (Corneille's *Cinna*), and Camille (Corneille's *Horace*). Her fellow actors were mediocre. "Some of them...irresistibly ludicrous," commented Miss Kemble. It was general practice for theatrical stars to appear with inferior colleagues who would not detract from their performance.

As in Paris, so in London, Rachel was "the rage" with royalty and society. "All the fine ladies and gentlemen crazy after her," related Fanny Kemble, "the Queen throwing her roses on the stage out of her own bouquet, and vicountesses and marchionesses driving her about."[24] Victoria invited the French tragedienne to perform at Windsor Castle and presented her with a gold and diamond bracelet inscribed: "A Rachel,

Victoria Reine." In order for the actress to stay in London for five additional performances, the Queen paid Rachel 15,000 francs to cancel her engagement in Marseille. Queen Victoria remained one of Rachel's most devoted admirers.

Rachel then returned to the Comédie Française. The following summer she performed in Brussels and was seen by Charlotte Brontë. The Victorian novelist was appalled by the tragedienne's personification of evil. In her novel *Villette*, she described Rachel's portrayal as follows:

> For a while - a long while - I thought it was only a woman, though an unique woman, who moved in might and grace before the multitude. By-and-by I recognized my mistake. Behold! I found upon her something neither of woman nor of man; in each of her eyes sat a devil. These evil forces bore her through the tragedy, kept up her feeble strength - for she was but a frail creature; and as the action rose and the stir deepened, how wildly they shook her with their passions of the pit! They wrote HELL on her straight, haughty brow. They tuned her voice to the note of torment. They writhed her regal face to a demoniac mask. Hate and Murder and Madness incarnate she stood. It was a marvelous sight; a mighty revelation. It was a spectacle low, horrible, immoral.[25]

In January 1843, Rachel undertook the role of Racine's Phèdre. She never ceased refining her characterizations and would alter actions until satisfied with the effect. The production had been rehearsed by Samson. After the opening, his pupil wrote: "I have studied my sobs [in the play's fourth act]. I do not dare to boast for the second representation; but I am sure they are coming. Not having seen you behind the scenes, I will make a point of looking at you as I come on, and will soon see if you are pleased."[26] The actress devoted 11 years to perfecting her interpretation of Racine's guilt-ridden heroine. Rachel's Phèdre was obsessed by a devouring passion. "Phaedra must be almost divine," stated Rachel's biographer Mrs. Arthur Kennard, "in her sorrow and her love. And it was from this point of view that Rachel so immeasurably surpassed all other actresses."[27] According to Théophile Gauthier, she appeared with "feet dragging, shoulders bowed, her body stooping, and her head fallen upon her breast, her draperies heavy and perpendicular, her eyes red in her mask of pale marble."[28] "Bending under the weight of her purple robes and her diadem," adds the authoress Madame Blaze de Bury, "...There is in the wan and wasted face of Mlle. Rachel something unearthly, an unnatural transparency, a sort of lighting from within,...her limbs totter... impatiently her unsteady hand strives to relieve her aching brow from the 'vain ornaments' that oppress and overload it!"[29] "In the second act where she declares her passion," wrote the English critic George Henry Lewes, "...It was terrible in its vehemence and abandonment; eloquent in its horror; fierce and rapid, as if the thoughts were crowding upon her brain in a tumult, and varied with such amazing compass of tones."[30] "Rachel was the mouth-piece of the gods," concluded Mrs. Kennard, " no longer a free agent, she poured forth every epithet of adoration that Aphrodite could suggest, clambering up higher and higher in the intensity of her emotion, whilst her audience hung breathless, riveted on every word, and only dared to burst forth in thunders of applause after she had vanished from their sight."[31] Not wishing to dispel the mood, the actress did not appear before the curtain at the play's conclusion.

By now, Rachel received the highest salary at the Comédie Française. Her annual six month vacations were devoted to performances in the French provinces and abroad. Aside from return engagements in England, she traveled to Prussia, Austria, Italy, Russia, and finally to the United States. The actress led a phrenetic existence, craving constant change and emotional excitement. Her lovers were numerous and varied, including Napoléon III and Dr. Louis-Désiré Véron, the debauched, obese, bald, and scrofulous owner of the newspaper *Revue de Paris* and Director of the Paris Opera. Rachel's love affairs were often brief. Despite her promiscuity, she demanded decorous behavior from her lovers. When a compliment was paid her because of Count Alexander Walewski's "manner of a visitor, rather than of a lover," the actress answered; "I am like that; I don't mind tenants, but I bar owners."[32]

She had two sons. One by Walewski was born in 1844, and the other in 1848 by Arthur Bertrand. Rachel drove herself mercilessly in order to support the children she adored as well as her rapacious parents, brother, and four sisters. In addition, she maintained a luxurious home which had been a gift from Walewski. Once when on tour, she wrote Véron: "What a tour! What fatigue! but what profit!"[33]

The actress, however, was suffering from tuberculosis which was aggravated by her frenzied life style. During a rehearsal for the premiere of *Adrienne Lecouvreur* in 1848, Rachel had a premonition of her own early death. Ernest Legouvé recalled of the last act:

> From the very beginning, something in Rachel's accent thrilled me to the heart. Never before had I seen her so truly, simply and affectingly tragic....The act over...I went up to her...saying ...'You have played that fifth act, my dear, as you will never play it again in all your life.' 'That is my own conviction,' she replied....'An exceedingly strange phenomenon took place within me. It was not over

Adrienne that I have been weeping, but over myself! Something suddenly told me that, like Adrienne, I should die young. I felt as if I were lying in my own room, at my last moment, present at my own death! And when I repeated the lines: 'Farewell, dramatic triumphs! Farewell, entrancing art that I have loved so much!' you saw me shed real tears. With mournful despair, I was rapidly realizing how soon time would sweep away every recollection of my little talents, and the world would soon be left with the faintest trace of poor Rachel.[34]

Adrienne became one of her most popular roles, proving that Rachel also was able to perform sympathetic characters. "Her expressions of tenderness," wrote Fanny Kemble, "though rare, were perfect."[35] But she seldom ventured into contemporary repertoire, accepting only those roles which she considered suitable to her style of acting. In refusing Legouvé's *Medea* in 1853, she explained: "I see my role is full of sharp, sudden movements; I rush at my children, carry them about, struggle with the crowd for their possession. This physical agitation does not suit me. All that I can express by physiognomy, attitude, by solemn, measured gesture, I can do; but where energetic pantomime begins my powers fail utterly."[36] Rachel was repelled by *Medea's* character, stating: "Medea may murder her children, poison her father-in-law: I feel unable to follow her example, even if I wished to!"[37]

In 1850, Rachel had been attracted to Tisbé in Hugo's *Angelo* and studied the role with the author. She was able to associate herself with the Renaissance actress-courtesan, stating:

You need to be like me, a poor child who has sung in the

streets, to begin to understand and interpret this Tisbé, this mixture of charm and prostitution, of fierceness and generosity, of lofty feelings amid a life of luxury and lust. Oh! what a strange thing this woman born in the gutter who wakes to find herself in sheets of satin! How scornfully and bitterly she looks upon the world that yesterday abandoned her in her purity, and to-day is prodigal of caresses in her dishonor![38]

One of Rachel's most stirring performances was not in a play. Theatres were empty in 1848 following Louis Philippe's abdication and the establishment of the Second Republic. Everywhere mobs were shouting the *Marseillaise*. After hearing them, Rachel devised a means of attracting the public back to the Comédie Française. "The *Marseillaise* is a fine thing," she said, "a hymn of passion; and I saw it as a chance to apply the art I'd studied all my life!"[39] Following a performance on March 6, 1848, Rachel appeared on stage dressed in white. According to contemporary accounts, the actress "seized" the tricolor flag "lying on a bench...and...holding it aloft, came towards the footlights, chanting, low and fierce."[40] "Her attitude, her gestures, the poses of her head expressed the meaning of each stanza to admiration. How proudly she raised her neck, free at last of the yoke!...What a wealth of accumulated hate, what a thrust of vengeance betrayed themselves in her clenched fists, in the nerves that pulsed beneath the cold immobility of implacable resolution! And with what tender effusion -- did she kneel and sink into the tricolour folds of the symbolic flag."[41] "A perfect delirium of excitement fell upon the crowd, ...Republicans fell sobbing into one another's arms; Royalists trembled and shivered before the great wave of Revolutionary exultation that swept around them."[42] During the remainder of March, Rachel repeated the performance 24 times to full houses.

In 1853, she undertook a tour of Russia and was entertained at St. Petersburg by Czar Nicholas I and his family. Rachel recorded of that evening:

> ...your humble servant was entertained like a queen. No sham tragedy queen with a gilt pasteboard crown, but a real queen, stamped with the stamp of the Royal Mint....a grand banquet given in my honour at the Imperial Palace. A...daughter of Papa and Mama Félix!...What splendour! Behold! at my arrival...great footman powdered and covered with gold lace, as in Paris...escorted me up-stairs. One took my cloak, another went in front and announced me, and I entered a drawing-room gilded from floor to ceiling, the occupants of which seemed...to rush forward to greet me. One of the Grand Dukes, a brother of the Emperor, conducted me to the dinner-table. An immense table, raised upon a dais,...laid for...only thirty; but what a select company! The Imperial family, the Grand Dukes, the little Dukes and archdukes....All this tra-la-la of princes and princesses, curious and attentive, never took their eyes off me for a moment, watching my every movement, every smile, and listening to every word I spoke. You must not think I was embarrassed; not the least in the world! My self-possession never forsook me for a moment until the middle of the repast, which , by the way, was very good; but everyone seemed more occupied with watching me than eating their dinner. At that moment the "toasts" in my honour began, and the scene that took place was a most

extraordinary one. The young archdukes, to get a better view of me, rose, mounted on their chairs, and ever put their feet upon the table--I was going to say into the plates! No one seemed astonished. Evidently there is still a great deal of the savage in the princes of this country. They shouted, cried "Bravo!" and called upon me to recite something. To reply to toasts by a tragic tirade was, indeed, strange; but I was equal to the occasion. I rose, pushed back my chair, assumed the most tragic air of my repertory, and rushed into the great scene in *Phèdre*. A death-like silence came over the company: you could have heard a fly, were there any in this country. They all listened religiously bent forward towards me with gestures of profound admiration. Then, when I had come to an end, there was a fresh outbreak of cries...clink of glasses and renewed toasts, to such an extent that I remained a moment quite overcome. Soon, however, the excitement took possession of me, the fumes of the wine, the scent of the flowers, all this enthusiasm, which certainly flattered my vanity, got into my head. I again rose, and began to sing, or rather declaim, the Russian National Hymn. On this it was no longer enthusiasm, but frenzy. They crowded round me, they pressed my hands, they thanked me. I was the greatest tragedian of all times past and future. Thus they went on for a good quarter of an hour.

But the best things come to an end at last; the hour struck when I must take my leave. I accomplished this with the same queenly dignity as when I arrived, conducted to the great staircase by the same Grand Duke, who, although gallant and attentive, never forgot his punctilious politeness. Then appeared the splendid powdered footmen, one of whom carried my cloak; I put it on and was escorted by them to my carriage, which was surrounded by other footmen carrying torches to light me on my way.[43]

In addition, she was presented with magnificent jewels by the Royal Family. The tour proved an immense success.

Rachel returned from Russia in 1854 completely exhausted, but 300,000 francs richer. In 1855, she was granted a leave of absence from the Comédie Française to perform in the United States. Fanny Elssler the Viennese ballerina and Jenny Lind the Swedish soprano had reaped fortunes in America. Phineas T. Barnum had brought the famous singer to the United States in 1850. In 1853, he had suggested a tour to Rachel, but she was uninterested at the time and refused his offer. Following her successful Russian tour, however, Rachel's brother Raphaël persuaded her to perform in America under his management.

For eighteen years, Rachel's faithful Parisian public had tolerated her frequent absences, but her departure from France at the time of the International Exhibition infuriated them. In addition, an intensely emotional Italian actress had arrived on the scene - the beautiful Adelaide Ristori. Rachel's enemies raved about this Italian performer. Alexandre Dumas *père*, whom Rachel had rejected as a lover, compared Ristori to Lecouvreur and Clairon. He advised the French star to attend one of Ristori's performances in order to learn from her acting. Even Janin was profuse in praise of the Italian actress. The Salle Ventadour, in which the Royal Sardinian Company performed, was filled with cheering Parisians.

Rachel saw Ristori as Mme. Delancour in Goldoni's comedy *Il burberino benefico* and as Alfieri's tragic Myrrha. She staged an immediate return to the Comédie Française for nine performances. Ristori attended her performances of Corneille's Camille and Racine's Phèdre. Later she wrote of Camille:

> She looked like a Roman statue! her majestic carriage, her regal bearing -- In the stupendous culminating scene, where we have the imprecation against Rome and the Romans, she uttered such accents of hatred, of rage, that the whole audience was frightened....She not only possessed genius for the stage, power of forceful expression, nobility of features, reality and nobility of pose; she also knew how to enter the life of the character that she represented, and she held herself in it from the beginning to the end of the play, without neglecting any details, producing majestically all of its great effects, and giving scrupulous attention even to the least noticeable.44

But Ristori had reservations about Rachel's Phèdre, stating: "The prostration which she showed seemed to me quite excessive, and moreover, she neglected to portray clearly that this prostration was only due to moral languor, which disappears when its intensity is removed, and allows the body to resume its vigour."45 And she thought that Rachel "exaggerated perhaps the impetus of too expressive realism"46 in her second act declaration of love to her stepson Hippolytus. Ristori's greatest success in Paris was as Alfieri's Myrrha, another woman consumed by incestuous passion. The Italian actress' view of Phèdre may have been colored by professional bias. Later her portrayal of the Grecian queen was significantly different from that of the French artist. "Rachel inspired terror," recalled the English critic Henry Morley, "Madame Ristori awakens pity."[47] Rachel emphasized Phèdre's evil, destructive nature. Ristori depicted a hapless "woman, who, crazy with love casts aside modesty, dignity, and all in order to obtain the satisfaction which her guilty passion causes her to desire."[48]

According to the press, Rachel's Phèdre had never been acted "with wilder, more furious passion."[49] But these fiery outbursts were interspersed with rapidly passed over portions of the play. Rachel was in the advanced stages of tuberculosis and needed to conserve her dramatic powers for the climactic tirades. With her final performances at the Comédie Française, Rachel won back the public which a few weeks before had spitefully withheld its applause at her entrance.

By now, Rachel's health was precarious. The actress tired easily and hallucinated. Before leaving for New York, she appeared in London. Then on August 10, 1855, she sailed for the United States from Liverpool.

She made her American debut as Camille on September 3 at Broadway's Metropolitan Theatre. The opening night was well attended and the press generous in their praise. "So deep, vibrant and magnetic were the first tones of that voice, "wrote a critic," that they sent a thrill through the vast assembly, a thrill which at once opened the communication between the genius of Rachel and her new hearers."[50] And in *Harpers Magazine*, the editor recorded:

> For an hour and a half, there was the constant increase of passionate intensity, until love and despair culminated in the famous denunciation; the house hung breathless upon that wild whirl of tragic force - and Camille lay dead, and the curtain was down,...The curtain rose, and there, wan and wavering, stood the ghost of Camille, the woman Rachel. She had risen in her flowing drapery just where she

had fallen ... pale and trembling, she flickered in the tempest of applause. The audience stood and waved hats and handkerchiefs, and flowers fell in pyramids;...It was a great triumph. It was too much for the excited and exhausted Rachel....She wavered for a moment. Then someone rushed forward and caught her as she fell - and the curtain came down.[51]

After the first performance, attendance waned because few Americans understood French. The audiences purchased translations of the plays and read them during the performances. It sounded like "the rain ...pattering," complained an actor, Léon Beauvallet, as "the whole audience" turned pages "simultaneously."[52] Many merely came to look at France's leading actress and left before the play was over. "Her magnificent diction, her wealth of expression, her admirable sense of movement and gesture, " commented Beauvallet, "all that was lost on them."[53] They only applauded "animated tirades, the scenes of action, when movements became quicker, gestures more lively, and the voice was raised above its customary level."[54]

Camille was followed by performances of Phèdre, Adrienne Lecouvreur, and Marie Stuart, but receipts were not as expected. Jenny Lind's first appearance in New York had netted $17,864; Rachel's only $5,016. Raphaël lacked Barnum's genius for publicity and sales. Tickets for Jenny Lind's concert had been auctioned to the highest bidders, while Rachel could be seen for normal theatre prices. Lind's art of song needed no translation. Rachel's demanded fluency of language. Jenny Lind was a model of Victorian respectability. Puritan-minded middle- and upper-class Americans refused to condone Rachel's notorious love affairs.

In October, Rachel traveled to Boston for nine performances. The audiences were enthusiastic. One evening Harvard College students appeared as supernumeraries in order to look at the famous actress. The company returned to New York in November for additional performances. They appeared first at the vast Academy of Music and then at the smaller Niblo's Garden. Later that month, Rachel and her troupe opened in Philadelphia at the Walnut Street Theatre. The French star was still suffering from a cough which had developed in New York. She caught a severe cold in the icy theatre and was confined to her hotel room while the company performed other plays without her. Rachel spent time reading the novels of James Fenimore Cooper. The tragedienne was a voracious reader, and her Paris home contained an extensive library.

At the end of November, Rachel set out for Charleston. On December 17, she appeared in the part of Adrienne Lecouvreur. Two days later, the company sailed for Havana, but Rachel had to cancel all performances. The actress returned to France early in 1856, never to act again. Rachel wrote of the tour to a friend:

> I cannot speak of it without weeping. But how could I foresee its fatal ending? I was so certain of success. And this terrible disease - this shirt of Nessus that I cannot tear off! I trusted to my luck and my strength, and, without any precautions, undertook this terrible expedition to New York....You, who knew Rachel so brilliant, who saw her in her luxury and her splendour, who so often applauded her in her triumphs - you would find a difficulty in recognizing her now in the skeleton that she drags about with her unceasingly.[55]

For eighteen years, Rachel epitomized the words she had spoken to her brother in 1843: "If your vocation leads you to the stage, try at least to raise the art of the theatre. Work conscientiously, not to make a position for yourself ... but rather from passionate love for the works that feed your spirit and guide your heart."[56] In October 1857, she left Paris for "the warmth and sunshine"[57] of the French Riviera. She died on January 3, 1858, in Le Cannet. Shortly before her death, the actress had told her sister Sarah: "All night I have been thinking of Polyeute. If you only knew what new and magnificent effects I have conceived."[58]

On January 11, her body was returned to Paris and buried in the walled Jewish ghetto area of Père-Lachaise cemetery. The funeral cortege consisted of 600 carriages, and more than 100,000 people lined the streets.

"Her eyes charged with lightnings,...her voice as it changes from melodious clearness to a hoarseness that makes one shudder," wrote George Henry Lewes, "the fire, the fury, and the terror ... she reminded us of a panther, beautiful yet terrible."[59] And Fanny Kemble reflected: "The impression she had left upon my mind is that of the greatest dramatic genius ... and the most incomparable dramatic artist I ever saw."[60]

CHAPTER SIX
RISTORI   1822-1906

Rachel's successor on the international scene was the Italian actress Adelaide Ristori. Ristori was born on January 29, 1822, at Cividale del Fiuli, Italy. Her parents Antonio Ristori and Maddalena Pomatelli were members of a traveling troupe of actors, the Covicchi Company. Ristori made her debut at the age of three months and by four-and-a-half years was performing leads in farces. At 12, she was engaged by the Giuseppi Moncalvo Company to perform children's parts. Two years later, she acted the title role in Silvio Pellico's *Francesca da Rimini*. Moncalvo would have made her leading lady at 15, but Ristori's father rejected the offer. Instead, she became the ingenue of the Royal Sardinian Company. Within three years, she was their leading lady at the age of 18. The tall, well proportioned, chestnut-haired performer was equally competent in comedy and tragedy.

From childhood, Ristori had been taught acting by her grandmother. Now she was the student of the actress Carlotta Marchionni. "I learned to distinguish and to delineate," she wrote, "the comic and the dramatic passions."[1] She attempted to combine the realism of French acting with "the vivacity and spontaneity of the Italian temperament,"[2] calling it "coloured naturalness."[3]

In developing her portrayals, Ristori related: "I meditated over each verse, minutely scrutinizing every conception, analysing every word, studying the expression of the eye and finally I succeeded in perceiving how that...character should be interpreted."[4] Once she had decided upon an interpretation, she strove "to reproduce true to life."[5] "I endeavour," she explained, "always to enter into the nature of the character I had to represent by studying the customs of the times and by making historical researches....to represent the physical and moral personalities of my characters,...identifying myself with the characters which I represented and from having become inspired by their passions."[6]

Ristori said of her preparation for the role of Paolo Giacometti's Maria Antonietta:

> The love I had for historical truth induced me to visit the 'Conciergerie' in Paris, which had been the last dwelling-place of the unhappy Queen of France. I still recall the painful impression made upon me by the sight of this cell. Filled with the subject, I was studying in the environment of the great tragic human drama. I seemed to see that resigned martyr of the French Revolution; and to hear around me her heart-rending sighs![7]

Her depiction of the death scene from Carlo Marenco's *Pia dei Tolomei* was based upon personal observation. The unfortunate heroine is a victim of malarial fever. While studying the part, Ristori happened "to witness" a death from that disease. "This desolating scene," recalled the actress, "fixed itself so profoundly upon my mind, that while it assisted me in reproducing faithfully the heart-rending death of Pia, portrayed as a matter of fact the poor woman I had seen die, and at every performance, the painful scene thus recalled, would appear and trouble me profoundly."[8] Although she meticulously prepared each role, Ristori never hesitated to change her actions even during a performance. "I would find suddenly some inspiration," she explained, "some effect which I never studied, but , which was more realistic, more vivid than before."9

Like Rachel, she frequented art galleries in order to observe posture, gestures, and costuming. Of a particular pose in her portrayal of Legouvé's Medea, she stated: "this attitude, with many others, I had adopted from my study of the stupendous groups of Niobe which are in the famous Uffizi Gallery of Florence."10 And her costume as Maria Stuarda was fashioned after Myten's painting of the queen's execution in 1587 at Fotheringay Castle.

In 1847, Ristori married the Marquis Giuliano Capranica Del Grillo. They had four children, two of whom survived. The marquis accompanied his wife on her theatrical tours of Italy. Gradually Ristori began to think of performing outside of Italy. "My object," she recalled in her *Memoirs*, "was to vindicate abroad the true artistic genius of the Italian stage, and to show that Italy is not only the 'Land of the Dead.'"11 The actress was fervidly patriotic. But she also was personally ambitious, wanting her "art" to be brought "to the consideration of all peoples."12 She decided upon a tour of France with the Royal Sardinian Company. Ristori wanted recognition in Paris, the world's acknowledged cultural center. On May 22, 1855, they opened in the French capital with *Francesca da Rimini* and Giraud's farce *I Gelosi fortunati*. The Italian star appeared in both productions. Francesca was followed by portrayals of Alfieri's Myrrha and Maffei's Maria Stuarda. The much publicized rivalry with Rachel and the praise of Dumas *père* and Janin aided in making Ristori's Paris season a resounding success.

Ristori's acting was the antithesis to Rachel's. The Italian performer's emotional style was "angular and almost always over empathetic."13 The French artist's cerebral mode was stately and controlled. Ristori excelled in the melodramatic tragedies of European romanticism. Rachel shone in the formal French classics. Ristori's movements and gestures were energetic and broad. Rachel's were "solemn" and "measured."[14] According to the American theatre critic William Winter, Ristori's "art methods were, distinctly rugged rather than delicate;...She ranked in the school of natural, as contrasted with the school of ideal, tragedians."[15] And William Macready referred to the "melodramatic abandonment"[16] of her acting.

Ristori's frequent histrionic exaggerations resulted from her passionate desire for realism. This is evident in the actress' written analyses of various roles. She described her actions in a scene from *Myrrha* as follows:

> The chest of Myrrha expands in an endeavor to repress and conceal the terrible tempest which rages within....At that point I transform the expression of my face, as if I were the prey of delirium,...with a quick turn of my person, I find myself face to face with my father who, with his arms on his chest, is looking at me in a threatening way. Struck by that glance, my blood grows chill, my courage fails and crying: 'Alas!' I fall upon the ground, as if struck by lightning.[17]

And of the confrontation scene between Mary and Elizabeth in Schiller's *Maria Stuart*, she wrote:

> Listening to such an outrageous insult, a flush of blood rushes to my face, and I act as if about to throw myself upon her,...then making a superhuman effort to control my wrath, I rapidly and convulsively press my rosary upon my chest,...At this point, I want to speak, but cannot, owing to

the paroxysm of rage, which has discoloured my face and caused my body to tremble all over. Then, with great difficulty and in a suffocating voice ... I begin my invective.

She concluded the speech "in a strong voice, and with darting glances" which revealed her "fury has reached its height."[18]

Following her Paris triumph, Ristori went on to further successes in Brussels, Dresden, and Berlin. The actress returned to Italy in November 1855. "Seeing me again," she stated, "the Italian public scarcely knew how to show its gratefulness to me for having succeeded in causing Italian art to be appreciated in foreign countries."[19] Italians regarded international renown as an asset, while the French resented it. Paris was a cultural mecca. Italy was an artistic backwater except for opera.

Adelaide Ristori formed her own company and was to prove an authoritarian actress-manager. She related: "All obeyed me. None questioned my authority ... I almost always met with courtesy among the actors under my direction, and if any one of them dared to trouble our harmony, he was instantly put to his proper place by the firmness of my discipline."[20]

On one occasion, her sense of discipline included the audience. When revolutionists disrupted the Italian premiere of Giacometti's *Maria Antonietta* at Bologna, Ristori marched downstage. Signaling for silence, she said:

Ladies and gentlemen, in producing ... this drama of our illustrious compatriot, I thought I acted wisely in selecting as its first judge a Bolognese audience, so renowned for its keen intelligence and acquired appreciation of the beautiful. I do not ask anybody to applaud what he does not like, but in

> order to be able to pass a true judgement upon a work of this kind it is necessary to see and to listen unbiased by party prejudice. Let all party feeling be forgotten then, and let the majority of this honorable audience who came here tonight unprejudiced by any political bias or aspiration, enjoy this historical and classic production according to its dramatic merits.[21]

The actress was hailed with "an outburst of applause," and order prevailed for the remainder of the evening.

In February 1856, Ristori's troupe toured to Vienna, Paris, and London. On April 8 at Paris' Salle Ventadour, the Italian actress created the role of Legouvé's Medea, which had been rejected by Rachel. At first, Ristori also had refused the part because of her "high sense of maternal love."[22] The actress claimed that she "could never even in fiction pretend to slay children on stage."[23] If roles were "either revolting or repugnant" to her "nature" or to her "individuality," she rejected them.[24] But Ristori finally consented to perform this role after learning that the murders would be hidden from the audience by a mob intent on taking away Medea's children. Also Medea's violence was mitigated by a passionate love for her sons. Thus she was a tragic rather than a vicious figure. The play was a success, and Medea became one of Ristori's most popular portrayals, noted for its "luxuriant animal vitality."[25] This was especially evident in the first act as the deserted Colchian sorceress swears to avenge herself like a leopard leaping upon its prey. Ristori wrote of her action: "I pronounce these...verses with the expression of a wild beast that is about to devour somebody, and making the gesture of tearing my victim to pieces."[26] She explained that "this attitude of ferocity seemed to me logical, not only owing to the nature of Medea, but to that of any woman possessing a strong temperament and capable of excesses either of love or of hate."[27] Her portrayal of Medea's hate epitomized the actress' concept of heightened realism. "My aspect is transformed," she said, "my limbs writhe, my eyes dart fire, my mouth appears as if pouring venom."[28]

In June, Ristori took her company to London for performances at the Lyceum Theatre. She was well received by the British public and press. The actress agreed to return in June 1857 for appearances as Lady Macbeth at Covent Garden. The production was to be staged by Augustus Glossop Harris "according to English traditions."[29] Harris was an obvious choice. As the Garden's manager for opera and ballet, he was fluent in Italian.

After an intensive study of the role, Ristori came to the conclusion that Lady Macbeth was "not a human being, but a creature worse than a wild beast"[30] and a "monster in human likeness."[31] She was convinced that "affection for her husband was the last factor actuating her deeds - that she was animated only by her excessive ambition to reign with him, and that,...she used her affection for him as a means to satisfy her ambition."[32] "That serpent," she added "becomes absolute mistress of this man, entwines him in her grasp, and no human power can even tear him from it."[33] In the first act Ristori's Lady Macbeth enticed her husband into submission after his return from battle. Ristori explained:

> I had the thought of inducing him to pass his left arm around my waist. In that attitude I take his right hand and placing his index finger upon my lips I charge him to be silent, in the meanwhile I am slowly pushing him behind the wings, his back turned to them. All this was executed with a mingling of sentiments and magnetising glances, which fascinations Macbeth could not very well resist.[34]

By the time of the sleepwalking scene, however, Ristori's Scottish queen "is eaten up by the remorse preying on her mind."[35] Ristori wrote:

> I enter the stage with the looks of an automaton, dragging my feet as if they wore leaden shoes. I mechanically place my lamp upon the table, taking care that all my movements are slow and intercepted by my chilled nerves. With a fixed eye [riveted on one point][36] which looks but does not see, my eye lids wide open, a difficult mode of breathing, I constantly show the nervous agitation produced by the derangement of my brain.[37]

The actress' eyes watered profusely after this scene, and the strain eventually resulted in weakened vision.

Ristori's Lady Macbeth was a ruthless Machiavellian villainess. Her portrayal won approval in England. It echoed Mrs. Siddons' powerful representation. Ristori even emphasized the words "shalt be" from the letter scene as had been done by her famous predecessor. When the Italian star learned of the coincidence, she claimed this proved that "Mrs. Siddons also understood the importance of analysing the missive, of weighing every sentence, in order to transmit to the public the mystic meaning."[38]

In September 1857, Ristori made her debut in Madrid. Queen Isabella became her avid supporter and attended every performance. One evening, before her appearance on stage, two strangers requested the actress' assistance. A young soldier had been condemned to death unjustly. They begged Ristori to intercede on his behalf with the Queen. Following the first act, Ristori paid a visit to the royal box and threw herself at the Queen's feet pleading for the young man's life. Isabella granted an immediate pardon. When the audience learned of the act, both women were greeted with rapturous cheers. Ristori recalled: "By gestures I tried to indicate that to her Majesty the thanks were due; while she, always thoughtful of me, cried: 'No, no, it is to her, it is to her!'"[39] In later years, the soldier attended Ristori's performances in Madrid and would shout: "Long live Ristori --- long live the Queen!"[40]

For the next three years, Ristori performed throughout Europe, and then in 1860 went to Russia. Four years later the actress visited Egypt and Greece. In Athens she toured the Acropolis and recorded: "I stood ecstatic ... studying the Greek reliefs in order to reproduce, at the first opportunity in my costumes, those stupendous folds."[41] And she declared: "What luck was it for me to find again among those sublime marbles all the noble poses that I had endeavoured to reproduce before my audiences."[42]

Ristori traveled to the United States in 1866, opening as Medea on September 20 at New York's Lyceum Theatre. Her debut was a success. "Her voice is wonderfully beautiful," wrote the *New York Tribune's* critic, "Her figure imposes, and her face, though far from being tragic ideal, is expressive and sympathetic....She is worlds in advance of any woman on the American or English stage."[43] The actress' Lady Macbeth, however, met with mixed reactions. The American biographer Edward Robins recalled: "It was the most unscrupulous of all our Lady Macbeths, and while we almost despised the character, for its rank callousness, we were lost in admiration for the actress."[44] While William Winter thought: "Her Lady Macbeth was a murderous Italian virago."[45]

But there was not a dissenting voice concerning her performance of Queen Elizabeth in Giacometti's *Elisabetta, regina d'Inghilterra*. It undoubtedly was the actress' finest portrayal. Ristori disliked the role because of Elizabeth's "animosity toward the unhappy Mary Stuart."[46] The pious Italian actress regarded the Scottish queen as a saintly martyr and her English cousin as a cruel and arrogant hypocrite. Ristori wrote of her characterization that "to be able to combine the haughtiness, the royal dignity, the transcendent genius, the dissimulation, the hypocrisy, and the most striking absolutism, with the frivolity, the futility of a woman, vulgar at times, at others a queen, to portray all these different traits in one nature is a most arduous task."[47] In Giacometti's drama, Elizabeth is torn between her love for the Earl of Essex and her passion for power. At the play's beginning, the Queen is still a vigorous woman. "At her first appearance on the scene," stated Ristori, "the carriage, the gesture, the tone of voice of Elizabeth should be those of a person familiar with the ordering of important state affairs, whose opinion is not to be disputed."[48] She then adds: "I took particular care to make it plain to the spectators that, in spite of the affection which Elizabeth at that time felt for the Earl of Essex, her haughty nature would, with her sarcasm and disdain, place all on the same level, whenever she supposed that any one of her favorites dared to raise his ambitious aspiration to the possession of her hand."[49] By the play's end, Elizabeth has become a senile old woman haunted by the executions of Mary Stuart and the Earl of Essex. Ristori said of the last scene:

> I imagine myself enshrouded in darkness, I see the white shadows of bleeding ghosts coming toward me. In order to escape from them and not be grasped by one of them I huddle up in my bed; but the heads which have been cut off from their bodies, seem to roll down at my feet, they terrify me, and becoming the prey of horrible spasms I again fall on my bed, asking with joined hands and suffocating voice, for mercy!...The delirium and the agony of death are taking hold of me. The remembrance of Essex comes to me; it

seems as if I saw him I would reach my arms to him as though to draw him to me and give him a forgiving kiss, and after a short struggle with death, I finally succumb, remaining there with glassy eyes, surrounded by my courtiers.[50]

Robins wrote of her death scene that it "was the very climax of tragedy."[51] The *New York Tribune* referred to "the terrible realism"[52] of her portrayal. "The haughty carriage," stated the American drama critic John Ranken Towse, "imperious address, fierce temper, blunt humor, masculine sagacity, petty vanity, and feminine jealousy, were all indicated with surpassing skill and blended into a consistent whole with finished artistry."[53] And William Winter concluded that Elizabeth was "her utmost of achievement."[54]

Ristori toured the United States until May 1867, and then returned in September for an additional nine months, part of which was spent in Cuba. The actress gave a total of 349 performances. Unlike Rachel's appearances, Ristori's were well attended. The Italian actress' private life was untainted by scandal. Her doting husband and devoted children were much in evidence. Like Isabella Andreini, Adelaide Ristori possessed respectability.

The Italian tragedienne was seen again in the United States seven years later during her world tour, which lasted from April 1874 to January 1876. In addition to North America, she appeared in Brazil, Argentina, Uruguay, Chile, Peru, Mexico, and Australia. The tour, consisting of 312 performances, proved highly lucrative.

In 1873, Ristori commenced performances of Lady Macbeth's sleepwalking scene in English for her British and later American audiences. Encouraged by the enthusiastic response, she seriously began to study the English language in 1880. She found the elimination of her native intonation an arduous task. Two years later, she performed the role of Lady Macbeth in English on July 3, 1882, at Drury Lane. Soon after, she appeared in an English version of Giacometti's *Elizabeth the Queen*.

In 1884, she performed both of these roles in the United States. "It cannot be said," wrote Edward Robins, "that she gained anything, in an artistic way, by learning English, well as she acquitted herself. A certain smoothness and sonority of voice which distinguished her use of the soft Italian vowels was absent when she recited in alien lines."[55] And another viewer commented: "she had a pronounced inflection, and it is extremely difficult to follow her through a long speech, especially when excitement causes her to speak quickly....It is always evident that she speaks a language with which,...she still lacks sympathy and a complete mastery of its subtleties."[56]

Ristori toured the United States and Canada for seven months, but her reception was greatly diminished from that of the preceding 20 years. Toward the end of her stay, she appeared in a production of *Macbeth* with the distinguished American actor Edwin Booth as her leading man. This was followed by a performance in English of Schiller's *Maria Stuart* with the German-speaking company of New York's Thalia Theater. Ristori wrote of the one rehearsal: "I took good care to have the words which were to precede my answers repeated to me in succession, endeavouring to retain their sound in my ear."[57]

By 1885, Ristori's artistic supremacy was being challenged by the fascinating French actress Sarah Bernhardt. The Italian star returned to her home in Rome and retired from the theatre.

In summarizing her career, William Winter wrote:

> She could express, in absolute perfection, the fury of a

woman scorned. Her manifestations of ferocity, the wild anguish of remorse, and the delirium of desolation were tremendous, alike in their effect and their depth. The roots of that art, however, did not strike the ideal. The springs of it arose in the earth....She was unquestionably, a great actress; she possessed many attributes, physical and mental, which made her one of the foremost women of her time, but she lacked the ineffable quality which has always been found to animate and hallow the highest forms of human genius.[58]

Adelaide Ristori was a superb performer, but she did not reach the artistic heights of Rachel. According to Fanny Kemble, Rachel "surpassed" Ristori in both "pathetic tenderness" and "power."[59] And the brilliant French actor Louis Delaunay stated: "The more it is given to me to hear Mme. Ristori, the more I regret Rachel. I continue to think that the restraint and, at the same time, passionate interpretation of Rachel, is more to be valued that the exuberance of the celebrated Italian artiste."[60]

Ristori complete her *Memoirs and Artistic Studies* in 1888 and for the next 18 years devoted her life to her husband, children, and Roman society. Her son was chamberlain and her daughter lady-in-waiting to King Victor Emmanuel III's mother, Queen Margherita. On her eightieth birthday in 1902, theatres throughout Italy performed in her honor. Commemorative medals were issued, and Victor Emmanuel paid her a visit. That night Ristori was the honored guest at Rome's Teatro Valle. The King and Queen were present, and all attendant aristocrats proffered her bows. Five years later on October 9, 1906, Adelaide Ristori died in Rome. Her funeral was attended by the Italian Royal Family and by Germany's Kaiser Friedrich Wilhelm II. The noted actor Tommaso Salvini presented the eulogy. Ristori was buried in the cemetery of Campo Verano.

CHAPTER SEVEN
BERNHARDT 1844-1923

Shortly before her death, Rachel visited the Grandchamps Convent at Versailles. Her pallor and shortness of breath were noticed by a young girl who felt "sorry for her" until a nun explained "that what she did was killing her, for she was an actress."[1] Within a few years, the youthful Sarah Bernhardt was to succeed Rachel as France's leading tragedienne.

Sarah Bernhardt was born in Paris on October 23, 1844. She was the illegitimate daughter of Julie Bernhardt, a Dutch demimondaine. Her father was a wealthy young man from Le Havre. He was soon replaced, however, by other lovers, and the child was sent to live with a nurse in Brittany. Eventually, the peasant woman married and moved to Paris. She took the little girl with her because Sarah Bernhardt's mother had left France with her latest admirer and could not be located.

One day, the five-year-old child saw her mother's elegant sister Rosine. Running to reach her aunt, she fell on the sidewalk, breaking an arm and injuring a knee. The little girl stayed with her aunt until her mother's return. The lonely, moody, affection-starved Sarah Bernhardt was subject to violent temper tantrums which obtained the desired notice of her indifferent parent. Three years later, she was placed in Madame Fressard's boarding school and then in 1853 became a student at the Grandchamps Convent. The highly emotional ten-year-old was fascinated by the dramatic ritual and mysticism of the Catholic Church. Although her mother was a Jewess, Sarah Bernhardt was baptized and confirmed a Catholic. She had fasted for a week prior to her confirmation. "I was pale and had grown thinner," she recalled, "and my eyes looked larger from my perpetual transports, for I went to extremes in everything."[2] After seeing a novice take the veil, she was determined to become a nun. In her autobiography, Bernhardt reminisced:

> I pictured myself lying down on the ground, covered over with a heavy, black cloth, with its white cross, and four massive candlesticks placed at the four corners of the cloth. And I planned to die under this cloth. How I was to do this I did not know. I did not think of killing myself, as I knew that would be a crime. But I made up my mind to die like this, and my ideas galloped along so that I saw in my imagination the horror of the sisters and heard the cries of the pupils and was delighted at the emotion which I had caused.

The future actress' fertile imagination was becoming evident!

At the age of 14, Sarah Bernhardt returned to her mother's home and the company of two younger sisters, Jeanne and Régina. Julie Bernhardt refused permission for her daughter to enter the convent at Grandchamps. In turn, Sarah Bernhardt rejected the prospective suitors proffered by her mother. Finally, a family council was called. Julie Bernhardt's paramour the Duke de Morny suggested that the young woman enter the Paris Conservatoire. Since she declined marriage, a career in the theatre offered a potentially lucrative alternative. Perhaps because of de Morny's influence, Sarah Bernhardt was accepted as a student of acting at the Conservatoire in 1860.

Following her audition, Daniel François Auber, Director of the

Conservatoire and prominent opera composer, told Bernhardt he regretted "that such a pretty voice should not be for music."[4] For the next two years, she studied with Élie, Provost, Regnier, Talbot and Rachel's teacher Samson. Bernhardt was a conscientious student obsessed with the desire "to become the first, the most celebrated, and the most envied of actresses."[5] She wrote of her teachers: "I very much preferred Regnier's lessons to any others. He...taught us to be natural in what we recited. ...Provost taught a broad style, with diction somewhat pompous but sustained. He especially emphasized freedom of gesture and inflection.... [Samson's] method was simplicity. Provost emphasized breadth; Samson exactitude."[6] Talbot she credited with her mastery of abdominal breath control. Sarah Bernhardt's studies at the Conservatoire instilled impeccable articulation, seamless vocal range, ability to sustain numerous lines of text in one breath, and superb verse speaking.

But she was contemptuous of Élie's deportment classes. The actress recalled:

> We marched along on tiptoes with heads up and eyelids drawn over our eyes as we tried to look down in order to see where we were walking. We marched along like this with all the stateliness and solemnity of camels. He then taught us to make an exit with indifference, dignity or fury....Then there was what he called 'l'assiette' which meant the way to sit down in a dignified manner, to let oneself fall into a seat wearily, or the 'assiette' which meant: "I am listening, monsieur; say what you wish.'...I did my utmost later on to forget everything he had taught me.[7]

She did, however, retain his axiom that "gesture should precede speech."[8] She later augmented this precept, stating that "expression ought to precede gesture, which in its turn precedes speech."[9] This was to become one of her major theatrical principles.

In 1862, through the intercession of the Duke de Morny, she was offered a contract at the Comédie Française. The slender, blue-eyed, blond, frizzy-haired young woman made her debut on August 11 as Racine's Iphigénie and was nearly paralyzed by stage fright. Bernhardt, like Rachel, was to be plagued by this problem throughout her career. The critic Francisque Sarcey recorded that "she holds herself well, and her enunciation is perfectly clear."[10] She next appeared as Scribe's Valérie and Henriette in Molière's *Les Femmes savantes*. Her performances were judged as "insignificant" by Sarcey. "She is a debutant," he wrote, "and among the number presented to us it is only natural that some should be failures."[11]

Then at the January 15, 1863 annual ceremony honoring Molière's birth, Sarah Bernhardt slapped the face of Madame Nathalie, a senior actress. Régina Bernhardt had accompanied her sister backstage and accidentally stepped on Madame Nathalie's train. The actress pushed her into a column, cutting the little girl's face, and Bernhardt retaliated in kind. Edouard Thierry, Director of the Comédie Française, demanded an apology to Madame Nathalie. Sarah Bernhardt refused and shortly thereafter resigned from France's National Theatre. Years later, however, she volunteered to perform at Mme. Nathalie's retirement benefit performance. Bernhardt was temperamental but not spiteful.

Soon she procured a contract at the Gymnase where Rachel had made her debut. Like her earlier counterpart, Bernhardt was to prove unsuccessful in comedy. The actress wrote of her role in Raymond Deslandes' *Un Mari qui lance sa femme*:

> Princess Dimchinka, a frivolous, foolish, laughing individual,...was always eating or dancing. I did not like this role at all. I was very inexperienced on the stage and my timidity made me rather awkward. Then, too, I had not worked for three years with such persistency and conviction to create now the role of an idiotic woman in an imbecile play.[12]

Bernhardt broke her contract with the Gymnase. For several years, she travelled abroad and had numerous love affairs. One was with the Belgian Prince Henri de Ligne, by whom she had a son on December 22, 1864. According to the actress' own account, the Prince asked her to marry him, but his family was outraged. They secretly sent the young man's uncle General de Ligne to dissuade her from accepting the Prince's proposal. She conceded to the General's request and informed her lover that she was returning to the stage. De Ligne left her.

There is an interesting sequel to this story. In 1887, Sarah Bernhardt found Henri de Ligne awaiting her backstage after a performance in Paris. When the surprised actress questioned his visit, the Prince replied:

> Why should I be the only person not to come and applaud Sarah Bernhardt?...you have become the foremost French actress. Decidedly, it is you who were right. The life which I offered you could not give you the happiness which you have found in the life you have made for yourself.[13]

He had never learned of her sacrifice.

The following day at lunch he was introduced to his son Maurice

Bernhardt. The Prince offered to adopt the young man and make him his heir, but Maurice Bernhardt refused, stating:

> Since my birth, my mother alone had brought me up, sometimes with great difficulty, and has made every sacrifice for me. Whatever I am, I owe only to her. The only way in which I can prove my gratitude is by remaining her son, and hers alone. Your offer is very flattering, but I prefer to call myself Bernhardt.[14]

The next morning, the tragedienne's son accompanied his father to the crowded Gare du Nord railroad station. Henri de Ligne, mentioning his title to a guard, asked for an escort to the train. Unimpressed, the man replied: "Do like everybody else. Stand in line and wait."[15] Then Maurice Bernhardt said: "Could you help us to get through at once? I am the son of Madame Sarah Bernhardt."[16] Quickly the guard replied: "In that case, follow me."[17] Within a few minutes they were at the train, and the young man said to his father: "You see, it is also a very good thing to be called Bernhardt."[18]

In 1866, Sarah Bernhardt became a member of the Odéon Theatre, which produced both classical and modern plays. The company's approach to the classics was less traditional than that of the Comédie Française. The actress was praised for her performance of Shakespeare's Cordelia. Then she "charmed"[19] the public with her graceful movement and mellifluous voice as the youth Zacharie in Racine's *Athalie*. Over a period of 59 years, Sarah Bernhardt was to be seen in 27 breeches' roles.

Aside from her appearance in classical dramas, Bernhardt also acted in two plays by George Sand. In *François-le-Champi* she performed the role of Mariette and in *Le Marquis de Villemer* the part of Baronne d'Arglade. Sand and Bernhardt became close friends. "I used to watch her with the most romantic affection," recalled the actress, "for had she not been the heroine of a fine love romance!"[20] Sand's lovers were numerous and had included Alfred de Musset and Frédéric Chopin. Bernhardt was acquiring a following among the writers, artists, and students of Paris' Left Bank bohemia.

In 1868, Sarah Bernhardt was cast as Anna Damby in a revival of Alexandre Dumas *père*'s *Kean*. Victor Hugo was in exile, and many of his supporters objected to the performance of a play by Dumas instead of by Hugo. They filled the auditorium on opening night jeering Dumas and his mistress Ada Montrin. "The curtain was drawn up in the midst of a veritable tempest," related Bernhardt, "bird cries, mewing of cats, and a heavy rhythmical refrain of 'Ruy Blas! Ruy Blas! Victor Hugo! Victor Hugo!'" She described her entrance as follows:

> I was wearing the eccentric costume of an Englishwoman in the year 1820. As soon as I appeared I heard a burst of laughter, and I stood still, rooted to the sport in the doorway. But the very same instant the cheers of my dear friends, the students, drowned the laughter of the disagreeable people. I took courage, and even felt a desire to fight. But it was not necessary, for after the second, endlessly long, harangue, in which I give an idea of my love for Kean, the house was delighted, and gave me an ovation.[21]

A reviewer corroborated Sarah Bernhardt's words, stating that "her vibrant voice, that stunning voice, moved the public. She had tamed it, like a little Orpheus."[22]

She was becoming famous for her silvery, crystal clear soprano speaking voice which the Odéon's manager Félix Duquesnel found so beguiling he would not let her read to him from a script she was recommending for production. "Your voice is treacherous," he said, "It makes charming poetry of the worst lines possible."[23] Duquesnel, however, did accept François Coppée's poetic play *Le Passant* in which Sarah Bernhardt performed the breeches' role of the youthful troubadour Zanetto. The play was performed 150 times, and Bernhardt's voice was compared to "the song of the nightingale...the sighs of the wind...the murmurs of the water."[24]

The actress "loved" the Odéon Theatre and later wrote:

> I...worked very hard. I was always ready to take anyone's place at a moment's notice, for I knew all the roles....The theatre was a little like the continuation of school. The young 'artistes' came there, and Duquesnel was an intelligent manager, and very polite and young himself....I used to think of my few months at the Comédie Française. The little world I had known there had been stiff, scandal-mongering, and jealous. I recalled my few months at the Gymnase. Hats and dresses were always discussed there, and everyone chattered about a hundred things that had nothing to do with art....At the Odeon...we thought of nothing but putting on plays, and we rehearsed morning, afternoon, and at all hours.[25]

By Fall 1870, however, all theatrical performances had ceased in Paris. France and Prussia were at war, and Napoléon III had surrendered at Sedan to Wilhelm Friedrich I. The shattered forces of France had retreated to the environs of Paris, and the city was surrounded by Prussian troops. Paris was to be under siege for 19 weeks. Sarah Bernhardt requested permission to set up a hospital for wounded French soldiers in the Odéon Theatre. For five months, she and her small staff cared for 300 men. One of the young soldiers was a student at the École Polytechnique. Bernhardt had given him her own room in which she occasionally rested when exhausted from nursing the wounded. She often stopped to visit with him. When he was returning to the front, the nineteen-and-a-half-year-old soldier requested an autographed photo of the actress. They were to remain lifelong friends. Upon news of her death in 1923, the former soldier, now Marshal Ferdinand Foch Commander in Chief of the Allied Forces in the First World War, "was one of the very first to come and salute the mortal remains of the woman who, fifty-two years before, had nursed him in the auxiliary military hospital at the Odéon."[26] With the bombardment of Paris, Sarah Bernhardt closed her hospital. On January 28, 1871, the French capital capitulated to the Prussians, and Napoléon III's monarchy was replaced by the Third Republic.

Sarah Bernhardt rejoined the Odéon company when the Paris theatres reopened in fall of that year. The popular author and republican exile Victor Hugo returned to Paris. His plays were revived and the Odéon began rehearsals for *Ruy Blas*. Bernhardt was cast as the tragic love-smitten Dona Maria, Queen of Spain. The young actress' performance at the premiere on January 26, 1872, catapulted her into stardom. Hugo knelt before her murmuring "Merci! Merci!"[27] and Sarcey wrote: "that languishing and tender voice, with its perfect delivery of rhyme so that not one syllable is ever lost."[28] The exceptional beauty of Bernhardt's voice led Hugo to proclaim at a banquet commemorating the play's one hundredth performance: "Mademoiselle, you have a voice of gold!"[29] This phrase was to be associated with the French star for the rest of her career.

As a result of her extraordinary success in *Ruy Blas*, Sarah Bernhardt was offered 12,000 francs per year by Emile Perrin, Director of the Comédie Française. When Charles-Marie de Chilly of the Odéon refused her demand for an annual salary of 15,000 francs, the actress broke her contact and returned to the House of Molière.

For the next two years, Bernhardt performed the roles of Dumas *père*'s Mlle. de Belle Isle, Beaumarchais' Cherubin, Racine's Andromaque, and Aricie (*Phèdre*), Octave Feuillet's Berthe de Savigny (*Le Sphynx*), and Voltaire's Zaïre. She disliked the part of Zaïre, a Christian maiden murdered by her jealous Moslem captor, and had requested release from the production. Perrin, however, remained obdurate, and the play opened on a sweltering August night. The melodramatically imaginative young tragedienne again envisioned her own death - this time on stage instead of on the floor of a convent chapel. She recalled:

> I was determined to faint, determined to vomit blood, determined to die, in order to enrage Perrin. I gave myself entirely up to it. I had sobbed, I had loved, I had suffered, and had been stabbed by the poignard of *Orosmane*, uttering a true cry of suffering, for I had felt the steel penetrate my breast; then falling panting, dying, on the Oriental divan, I had meant to die in reality, and dared scarcely move my arms, convinced as I was that I was in my death agony and somewhat afraid, I must admit, at having succeeded in playing such a nasty trick on Perrin. But my surprise was great when the curtain fell at the close of the piece, and I got up quickly to answer to the call and salute the public without languor, without fainting, ready to

recommence the piece.[30]

Until this moment, Sarah Bernhardt had regarded her health as precarious because of recurring dizzy spells and oral hemorrhages. She had accepted the verdict that her "voice was pretty, but weak," her gestures "gracious, but vague," and her "supple movements lacked authority."[31] She now realized that her "physical strength" was equal to her "brain's conceptions,"[32] and she "resolved to be strong, vivacious, and active."[33]

It was at this point in her career that Sarah Bernhardt was cast as Racine's Phèdre. She was to substitute for the actress Roselia Rousseil and had only a few days to prepare for her debut on December 21, 1874, in the most challenging female role of French classical drama. She sought the advice of her colleague and former teacher Regnier. He counseled the young artist to emphasize sorrow or pathos rather than frenzy or fury in her characterization. Heeding his advice, Bernhardt presented Phèdre as "the most appealing, the purest, the most unfortunate victim of love."[34] She did not regard the Grecian queen as either "a termagant or a neurotic fury."[35] According to the English actress May Agate, Bernhardt

> refused to play the part demoniacally, concentrating firmly on the idea that the love of Phèdre for Hippolyte was a very human and genuine emotion, even if were not a permissible one. Her performance had none of Rachel's terror and evil in it....Without diminishing its stature, she reduced this remote Greek figure ... to simple terms of everydayness and brought the character before us as vividly as if she were a woman faced with the same torturing passion to-day....Phèdre in Madame Sarah's hands became any

woman driven to her doom by a fatal, inescapable complex....what did stand out a mile in her interpretation was the almost abnormal *sense* of *guilt* from which Phèdre suffered. Here was the cause of her physical weakness, the gnawing of the mind, the agony of self-accusation.[36]

These words were echoed by another viewer who wrote that Sarah Bernhardt "softened by nobility and beauty a part which her great forerunner had made almost unbearably horrible. Rachel had been an incarnate devil, Sarah was...a noble nature in overthrow."[37]

Bernhardt's interpretation was psychologically realistic, while Rachel's was classically mythological. Sarah Bernhardt's Phèdre was consumed with lust for her stepson Hippolyte, and her sexually motivated characterization was marked by seductive feline grace and femininity. She writhed and grasped her inner thighs, overwhelmed by the passion Phèdre attempted to conceal. The actress wrote of this moment:

It escapes from her in her cry of revolt against the gods....In saying more than she intended, she has betrayed herself. A more experienced man would have understood her cry of despair, but Hippolyte unwittingly furnishes her with arguments which will insensibly lead to her confession. And gradually hypnotized by the present reality of the dream which has haunted her every hour of her life for months, she loses consciousness of people and places, she speaks like a somnambulist; and repeats aloud all that she has murmured during her agonies of insomnia. Hippolyte's exclamation recalls her to herself; she stammers. And beside herself with shame and wounded, she cries out the truth, and asks for death at the hand of him whom she offended while adoring him.[38]

Miss Agate recalled that Bernhardt "made that one word 'Donne' ['Give'] last long enough to hurl herself at Hippolyte, clutch at his right shoulder with her left hand, and positively scrabble for his sword with her right arm across him, the whole in a frenzy of despair."[39] Once, the French star was so absorbed in her part, she was unaware until the scene's end that the sword's blade had cut deep into her hands. "This is nature itself," commented Sarcey of her portrayal, "served by a marvelous intelligence, by a soul of fire, by the most melodious voice that ever enchanted human ears. This woman plays with her heart, with her entrails."[40]

There were those, however, who found Sarah Bernhardt's libidinous portrayal too naturalistic. They preferred Rachel's interpretation of statuesque, demonic passion. Mrs. Arthur Kennard wrote:

> Sarah Bernhardt who in this role has most nearly approached [Rachel], is weak, unequal....We see all the viciousness of 'Phèdre' and none of her grandeur. She breaks herself to pieces against the huge difficulties of the conception, and does not succeed in moving us. In the second scene, where 'Phèdre,' thinking her husband is dead, confesses her incestuous passion to the object of it, Sarah Bernhardt never rises above the level of an Aventurière or a Frou-Frou.[41]

And Matthew Arnold replied to his niece's paeans for Bernhardt's performance: "But, my dear child, you see - you never saw Rachel!"[42]

Sarah Bernhardt, like Rachel, never ceased refining a portrayal. For many years she was to hone the role of Phèdre until it became her finest impersonation.

In 1877, Bernhardt won the hearts of both the playwright and the Parisian public for her performance of Dona Sol in Hugo's *Hernani*. Victor Hugo maintained that hers was the definitive portrayal of the hapless Spanish aristocrat. In appreciation, he presented the actress with a diamond drop representing the tears he had shed that evening.

Sarah Bernhardt was now the leading actress of France, but she was bored with her leisurely schedule at the Comédie Française. She took up sculpture and later painting. The actress thrived on publicity and soon became noted for her eccentricities, with a home inhabited by dogs, cats, monkeys, and even a lion. She had a skull inscribed with verses by Victor Hugo and kept a coffin in her bedroom. By the late 1870's, Sarah Bernhardt's daily activities were common knowledge throughout France.

Despite her numerous successes, Bernhardt resented the restrictive rules and traditions of the Comédie Française. "Oh those traditions!" she later wrote, "How many enthusiastic and sincere actors have found themselves fettered by them."[43] She recalled: "All the faults that were imputed to me when I played Phèdre for the first time....There were traditions which one could not resist under pain of being broken."[44] Then in 1879, she was censured by the Comédie Française for absence without leave from the French capital when riding in a balloon which strayed beyond the environs of Paris. Bernhardt, now referred to as *Mademoiselle Révolte*, promptly resigned. Emile Perrin lured her back, however, offering to make her a Sociétaire, or full member of the company, an honor conferred only after years of service. France's National Theatre was to visit London for a season at the Gaiety Theatre under the management of John Hollingshead. Sarah Bernhardt's fame was by now known abroad. Hollingshead would have withdrawn his offer if the French star were no longer a member of the company, even insisting that she appear on opening night. The Comédie Française was scheduled to perform two comedies by Molière featuring the company's senior members. Perrin arranged for Sarah Bernhardt to appear between the two works in the second act of *Phèdre*. Favoring an individual performer violated the no-star system of France's National Theatre. Much of Paris' public and many of the actress' colleagues were outraged!

Bernhardt wrote of her London debut on June 4, 1879:

> Three times over I put rouge on my cheeks, blackened my eyes, and three times over I took it all off again with a sponge. I thought I looked ugly, and it seemed to me I was thinner than ever and not as tall. I closed my eyes to listen to my voice. My special pitch is *le bal*, which I pronounced low down with the open a, *le baaal*, or that I take high by dwelling on the l-*le balll*. Ah! but there was no doubt about it, my *le bal* neither sounded high nor low, my voice was hoarse in the low notes and not clear in the soprano. I cried with rage, and just then I was informed that the second act of "Phèdre" was about to commence. This drove me wild. I had not my veil on, nor my rings, and my cameo belt was not fastened.
>
> I began to murmur:
>
> "Le voici! Vers mon cœur tout mon sang se retire.
> J'oublie en le voyant..."
>
> That word *j'oublie* struck me with a new idea. What if I did forget the words I had to say? Why, yes...What was it I had to say? I did not know... I could not remember...What was I to say after *en le voyant*...?

No one answered me. Everyone was alarmed at my nervous state. I heard Got mumble, "She's going mad!" Mlle. Thenard, who was playing *Œnone*, my old nurse, said to me: "Calm yourself, all the English have gone to Paris, there's no one in the house but Belgians."

This foolishly comic speech turned my thoughts in another direction. "How stupid you are!" I said. "You know how frightened I was at Brussels!"

"Oh, all for nothing!" she answered calmly. "There were only English people in the theater that day."

I had to go on the stage at once, and I could not even answer her, but she had changed the current of my ideas. I still had stage fright, but not the fright that paralyzes, only the kind that drives one wild. This is bad enough, but it is preferable to the other sort. It makes one do too much, but at any rate, one does something.

The whole house had applauded my arrival on the stage for a few seconds, and as I bent my head in acknowledgment, I said within myself: "Yes...yes...you shall see. I'm going to give you my very blood...my life itself...my soul...."

When I began my part, as I had lost my self-possession, I started on rather too high a note, and when once in full swing I could not get lowered again, I simply could not stop. I suffered, I wept, I implored, I cried out, and it was all real. My suffering was horrible, my tears were flowing - scorching and bitter. I implored *Hippolyte* for the love which was killing me, and my arms stretched out to Mounet-Sully were the arms of *Phèdre* writhing in the cruel longing for his embrace....God was within me --

When the curtain fell, Mounet-Sully lifted me up inanimate and carried me to my dressing-room.[45]

Sarah Bernhardt was an immediate success with the London audience and critics. She "held them spellbound,"[46] recorded Sir George Arthur. The English public did not seem to notice her hurried delivery and even idolized her later when she left out a key scene in Dumas fils' *L'Etrangère* because of a memory lapse. Bernhardt was learning that foreigners could be captivated by her superb pantomime and beauty of voice.

The French star was feted by London society and received large fees for reciting at aristocratic homes. Also her paintings and sculpture were exhibited and sold to wealthy purchasers. Both the recitals and exhibition had been arranged by the famous theatrical and musical manager Edward Jarrett. He suggested an American tour to Bernhardt, which she rejected at the time.

Upon her return to Paris, she was treated coolly by the public which resented her success abroad. At the annual homage to Molière ceremony on the stage of the Comédie Française, Sarah Bernhardt stepped towards the footlights and confronted the audience with a steady look. After a few moments, the Parisians capitulated and welcomed her back with a tumultuous ovation.

Soon, however, it was evident that Bernhardt did not intend to remain at the Comédie Française. Her success in London had revealed the possibility of international renown. The distinguished English actress Ellen Terry had seen the young French star and later recorded: "Even then I recognized that Sarah was not a bit conventional, and would not stay long at the Comédie."[47] Sarah Bernhardt, like Adelaide Ristori before her, yearned for world recognition and in 1880 resigned for the second time from the Comédie Française. "The Comédie Française," she afterwards stated to her granddaughter, "is and always will be the standard-bearer of the dramatic art of our country. I may have refused to serve in its ranks. Am I a deserter because of that? No. My own role was, perhaps, to make that standard float in the air of other countries, to make it known beyond the frontiers of France."[48]

Sarah Bernhardt formed her own company and opened at London's Gaiety Theatre with *Phèdre, Hernani, L'Etrangère,* and *Adrienne Lecouvreur.* Even the often critical French press acknowledged the excellence of her acting. Soon she signed a contract with Edward Jarrett to tour the United States that year.

During the Atlantic crossing in October 1880, Bernhardt was involved in a fascinating incident. She related:

> On the fourth day I dressed at seven o'clock and went on deck to have some fresh air. It was icy cold and as I walked up and down I met a lady dressed in black with a sad, resigned face. The sea looked gloomy and colorless and there were no waves. Suddenly a wild billow dashed so violently against our boat that we were both thrown down. I immediately clutched hold of one of the benches, but the unfortunately lady was flung forward. Springing to my feet with a bound I was just in time to seize hold of the skirt of her dress, and with the help of my maid and a sailor, we managed to prevent the poor woman from falling head first down the staircase. Very much hurt, though, she was, and a trifle confused; she thanked me in such a gentle, dreamy voice that my heart began to beat with emotion.

"You might have been killed, madame," I said, "down that horrible staircase."

"Yes," she answered, with a sigh of regret, "but it was not God's will. Are you not Madame Hessler?" she continued, looking earnestly at me.

"No, madame," I answered, "my name is Sarah Bernhardt."

She stepped back and drawing herself up, her face very pale and her brows knitted, she said in a mournful voice, a voice that was scarcely audible: "I am the widow of President Lincoln."

I, too, stepped back, and a thrill of anguish ran through me, for I had just done this unhappy woman the only service that I ought not to have done her - I had saved her from death. Her husband had been assassinated by an actor, Booth, and it was an actress who had now prevented her from joining her beloved husband. I went back again to my cabin and stayed there two days, for I had not the courage to meet that woman for whom I felt such sympathy, and to whom I should never dare to speak again.[49]

The advance publicity for Sarah Bernhardt's arrival in New York City was enormous. On October 27, ships with reporters, French consular officials, and distinguished New Yorkers sailed out to greet the famous actress. In order to escape the press' persistent questions, Bernhardt feigned a faint into Jarrett's arms. In the evening she attended the play *Alixe* by Prevois and Barrière, starring Clara Morris the American "Queen of Spasms." Miss Morris was noted for the realism of her death scenes, and her adoring public "flood[ed] the theatre with tears and almost drown[ed] out the action with [their] sobs."[50] Miss Morris came on stage armed with a bouquet which she tossed along with a kiss to Sarah Bernhardt. Madame Bernhardt pressed the flowers to her bosom and in turn threw a bouquet and a kiss to Clara Morris. The audience was enraptured.

Sarah Bernhardt opened on November 8 in Scribe's *Adrienne Lecouvreur*. The enthusiastic audience roared its approval while the French star took 27 curtain calls. New Yorkers were captivated by her frail appearance, feline grace, and beautiful voice. A few days later, she appeared in the role of Marguerite Gauthier from Dumas *fils*' *La Dame aux Camélias*. At first her managers Jarrett and his partner Henry Abbey suggested she drop the play from her repertoire since the press and clergy had declared the work immoral. Bernhardt was enraged and threatened a return to Paris if not permitted to perform in this play. "When Sarah Bernhardt arrived at the theatre that night," recalled a member of her company, "she was astonished to see huge red placards outside, announcing that she would play *Camille*. She rushed to Jarrett, the first man she met on the stage. 'What is it, this *Camille*?' she exclaimed furiously. 'I know no *Camille*!' 'Oh yes, you do,' said Jarrett, smiling urbanely. '*Camille* is--*La Dame*!' 'Oh!' cried Sarah and burst into uncontrollable laughter."[51] Abbey had decided to change the play's name, stating: "They will never know the difference."[52] *Camille* was to become her most popular role in America.

According to the American actress Cornelia Otis Skinner, "the secret of Bernhardt's success was in the disarming simplicity of her approach. She played Marguerite Gauthier with an exquisite frailty, a poetic pathos that was almost unbearable."[53] She minimized the clinical aspects of the heroine's illness, merely touching her lips lightly with a handkerchief to indicate tuberculosis. "As an artist," wrote William Winter, "she was above the medicine-chest and the slop-bowl."54 The public wept aloud after her death in the last act. The British artist Graham Robertson reported of that scene:

> The change that came over the face of the dying woman when she heard of her lover's coming was a nightly miracle to which I never got accustomed. I have often watched it from the side, at about 4 yards distance, but it was no trick of the stage. There was first a quick look at the bearer of the news, then the haggard face began to glow, the skin tightened all over it, the pupils of the eyes dilated, nearly covering the iris and darkly shining, the rigid lips relaxed and took soft childish curves, while from them came a cry that close at hand sounded no louder than a breath yet could be heard in the uttermost corner of the theatre. The frail body seemed to consume before your eyes in the flame of an unbearable joy to set free the glorified and transfigured spirit.55

May Agate also referred to "the cry with which she greeted Armand's return. That cry, which started in pure joy and ended in a sob, held in all the felicity and pain of love."56

Her acting in the last act was so realistic that one evening an elderly doctor accompanying Miss Agate to a performance "kept commenting on the criminal folly of allowing a tubercular patient to have visitors - for him the very atmosphere was germ-laden, and he kept repeating 'Everything she touches is infected.'"57 Sarah Bernhardt was to perform the role of Marguerite Gauthier hundreds of times over the next 30 years. Her characterization was perfected to such a degree that May Agate was to write of her acting:

> I must have seen this last act twenty times and, upon occasion, my mother and I have been in her dressing-room up to the moment of her call. So I knew perfectly well that there was no amateurish business of having to think herself into a sense of illness immediately before the scene - that had been done years before. Yes, I knew that she just switched into it, as easily as one turns on an electric fire! Yet everytime I saw this last act of *La Dame* I was convinced anew. Perfect technique is, of course, the explanation.[58]

This same "perfect technique" was described by the French actress Thérèse Berton who performed the role of the maid Nanine during a performance in Madrid of *La Dame aux Camélias*. Madame Berton lost her way in the backstage area of the immense Théâtre de l'Opera and missed an entrance. Bernhardt was furious, and according to Thérèse Berton:

> As she sank with glazing eyes on her couch I was amazed to hear her launch into a perfect stream of low-toned vituperation, directed at myself....'You ugly cow! This is not the proper garment!'...I was in such a nervous state that I had chosen the wrong garment....She kept up her death scene, taking twice as long as usual, because she kept thinking of new reproaches to hurl at me....finally, when she uttered a really outrageous insult - it was with her supposedly last breath that she said it - I leaned down, and, making the motions of intense and tearful grief, hissed

between my sobs: 'You say another word and I'll smack your face here on the stage!' I meant it too, and Sarah must have seen that I did, for she 'died' properly this time, and never pronounced another word. And all this while there was an audience out in the mistiness beyond, tense and grief-stricken, held by the marvelous acting of the great tragedienne on her stage death bed![59]

Sarah Bernhardt's American tour was both an artistic and a financial success earning the French artist over $500,000. Clergymen's denunciations of "her art" as "an inspiration from hell"[60] roused public interest in her performances. And she generated the usual publicity with her daily activities, including visits to Thomas Edison's laboratory in Menlo Park, New Jersey, a pig-slaughtering house in Chicago, Iroquois Indians in Canada, and a dead whale in Boston harbor. Over the next 36 years, she was to tour the United States eight more times.

When Bernhardt returned to Paris, the public again received her coldly. On July 14, 1881, there was to be a gala performance at the Opéra, followed by the tragedienne Marie Agar's recitation of the *Marseillaise*. Agar's maid was an avid admirer of Sarah Bernhardt. The two conspired to have her inform her mistress on the morning of the 14th that her lover was seriously ill in Tours. Agar immediately left for the south of France. Bernhardt's grandson-in-law Louis Verneuil recorded:

> That evening, about a quarter past eleven,...Sarah Bernhardt suddenly appeared, wrapped in a large cape with a hood, in the wings of the Opéra....
> 'What about Madame Agar?' one of the managers asked.
> 'Oh, that's true; I was forgetting. She had to leave Paris an

hour ago, having been called urgently to the bedside of a sick friend. She sends her apologies and has asked me to take her place. I need hardly say that I am very glad to do so....'

Then, perfectly at ease, Sarah Bernhardt appeared with a flag in her hand, and slowly advanced to the middle of the stage....Having voluntarily waited a few moments, during which a glacial silence reigned, Sarah Bernhardt, in a half whisper and an almost toneless voice, slowly began to enunciate the simple and sublime verses....

In an instant the three thousand members of the audience were seized with an indescribable emotion....

The enthusiasm was beyond description. The audience shouted: 'Bravo! Sarah! Sarah!...'

In a quarter of an hour Sarah Bernhardt had turned Paris around and had regained all her old popularity.[61]

For many years, Marie Agar had been a good friend of Sarah Bernhardt and laughingly forgave the two conspirators.

Bernhardt soon set forth on a tour of Belgium, Holland, Scandinavia, Russia, Austria, and Italy. In Russia, she acquired a handsome new leading man, the former Greek diplomat Jacques Damala. She married him in 1882, but the marriage was a failure. Damala was flagrantly unfaithful and an incurable drug addict. In addition, his good looks did not compensate for his inability to act. On December 12, 1882, Sarah Bernhardt opened in Victorien Sardou's *Fédora* with Pierre Berton as her leading man. Sardou had refused to cast Bernhardt's husband in the role of Ipanoff. Damala was furious and within a few days deserted the famous star.

For the next 20 years, Sardou was to create a series of historical romances tailored to the volcanic temperament of the French actress. *Fédora, Tosca, Cléopâtre, Gismonda,* and Th*éodora* consist of simple plots with text of secondary importance to self-explanatory actions. These melodramatic works concern fallen women, sex, and murder. All conclude with obligatory theatrical death scenes for which Sarah Bernhardt became noted. The actress' magnificent voice and dramatic actions were sufficient to enthrall foreign audiences.

In 1891, Bernhardt embarked on a tour of the United States, Canada, South America, and Australia. Then she commenced a series of productions at Paris' Théâtre de la Renaissance. In 1899, she leased the Théâtre des Nations and renamed it the Théâtre Sarah Bernhardt. There, for 16 years, she produced and starred in 40 productions, including Rostand's *l'Aiglon*. Bernhardt enjoyed performing breeches' parts. She had been seen as Coppée's *Zanetto*, de Musset's *Lorenzaccio*, and Shakespeare's *Hamlet*. "It is not male parts," she explained, "but male brains that I prefer."[62] Her greatest triumph in a male role was as l'Aiglon, the Duke of Reichstadt, Napoléon Bonaparte's son by Princess Marie Louise of Austria. Bernhardt's slender figure appeared to great advantage in elegant white uniform, tasseled sash and knee-high riding boots. The play concluded with a 20-minute emotional death scene.

The year 1905 saw Sarah Bernhardt begin a tour of the United States under the Schubert Brothers' management. Nearly all of America's theatres and opera houses were controlled by a theatrical syndicate composed of the powerful managers Sam Nixon, Fred Zimmerman, Charles Frohman, Al Hyman, Marc Klaw, and Abe Erlanger. The Schuberts were forced to book Sarah Bernhardt into ice rinks, an open-air theatre, and even a transportable tent. She also gave a performance at San Quentin prison.

In addition, she had toured South America for three and a half months. During a performance of *Tosca* on October 9, 1905, in Rio de Janeiro, Bernhardt suffered a severe injury. After leaping from the parapet at the play's conclusion, she missed the padded mattresses and her right knee slammed against the stage floor upon landing. Walking became difficult, and eventually she needed to lean on fellow actors for support. By 1913, stage furniture had to be so arranged that she could brace herself inconspicuously. Finally in 1915, the 70-year-old actress' leg was amputated. Sarah Bernhardt refused to wear an artificial limb and was transported in a litter chair.

Following her convalescence, she toured the front lines during the First World War reciting for the French troops. The elderly actress was accompanied by Béatrix Dussane, a young comedienne at the Comédie Française, who recalled:

> ...One day we were told that Sarah had expressed a wish to play to the soldiers.
>
> I had never met her before. I went to the Boulevard Pereire and, over the fire, in a white boudoir, I saw an extraordinary creature huddled in the depths of a low easy-chair; it consisted of thousands of folds of satin and lace surmounted by a reddish mop. It was an upsetting, rather depressing, sight; the great, brilliant Sarah seemed so small and helpless!
>
> But it was then, however, that I, as so many others before me, learnt something of her magic. For two hours she held forth, ordered tea, enquired about travelling conditions, got carried away, excited, amused; seeing everything, understanding everything, hearing everything.

And all the time she never stopped scintillating.

And now for our journey. Ah! The Gare de l'Est during the war, with our strange procession passing through it. Sarah, muffled in a striped coat with a large flowered hood, curled up in her little carrying-chair and smiling at everyone as if to dare them to pity her.

We got out at Toul, the only civilian party on the train. The little chair reappeared; it was painted white and decorated with Louis XV scrolls; even the chair seemed to smile, and to wish to appear a whim and not a painful necessity. The townspeople looked at her with so much curiosity and excitement that they forget to cheer or to applaud. Less than an hour later the cars came to take us to the scene of our first performance; a huge open market square in Commercy. There was a stage, with footlights and a curtain, but the place reserved for Sarah had no floor but the beaten earth; the stage could only be reached by a ten-rung ladder and the place was full of draughts. Sarah installed herself in her makeshift dressing-room and declared herself enchanted with everything.

At last her turn came to appear. While she was being settled on the stage, behind the curtain, in a rickety armchair filled with cushions, and we grouped ourselves around her, one of the Company went before the curtain and announced to the three thousand lads packed together in the square that they were about to see Sarah Bernhardt, which was a complete surprise to them.

The curtain rose, disclosing for us in the gloom beyond the bright light of the footlights first the stretcher-bearer musicians, then the wounded, whose white bandages riveted our eyes, and finally the multitude of eager-eyed faces. The ovation? It hung fire. There was a little applause, fairly warm but not unanimous and certainly not prolonged.

Sarah felt a shudder go through her. This audience meant more to her than any audience at any big first night. She began to speak. I was there, quite close to her. I neglected my own part and I looked at her. I knew almost by heart what she was going to say. But she made me forget it. Everything seemed to vibrate and, in a rhythm that rose like a bugle-call, she sang of the martyrdom of Rheims and of Belgium. She conjured up all the glorious dead of our race and ranged them beside the men fighting France's battles at the moment; the rhythm of her speech rose in a constant crescendo. It carried us away with Sarah, and when, on the last cry of '*Aux Armes!*' the band broke into the *Marseillaise*, the three thousand French lads cheered her to the echo.

This went on for three days; on a château terrace from which, in the distance, wrapped in mist but facing us, we could see the enemy positions at Woevre; in a hospital ward; in a ruined barn where the men even perched on the rafters. In all these places I witnessed Sarah's genius and her courage. No, we were never shelled. That was not the point. It was her courage as a cripple for whom will-power takes the place of all else, every hour of the day. We used to go out by car at about midday and return very late in the evening. Even when we stopped for meals we worked. Our dressing-rooms were casual hovels with straw-bottomed chairs or wooden trestles, the overpowering heat of a tent in the sun or the dampness of a cellar. On one occasion I found myself alone with her, and I had to help her to dress. She went from her chair to her dressing-table, leaning on me and hopping on her single seventy-year-old leg, which had the spareness of a bird's leg without its solidity. And she said to me, with a laugh:

'I'm like an old hen!'

It was marvellous to see that pluck which ignored her disability, her victory over ever-growing weakness, and pity turned to admiration.[63]

Sarah Bernhardt's lifelong motto *Quand Même* [Even Though] was indeed appropriate. For her wartime activities, she received the Legion of Honor - France's highest decoration.

After the war, she toured the United States, England, and Europe, performing one-act plays in theatres, music halls, and vaudeville houses. In 1920, she appeared in an act of Racine's *Athalie*. As she spoke the lines referring to an elderly woman applying makeup "to repair the years' irrepairable ravages," the public leapt to its feet in spontaneous applause. In response, Bernhardt courageously arose on one leg, balanced herself with a hand on her throne, and with a graceful wave of the other arm acknowledged the tribute. Later that year, she appeared in the role of Louis Verneuil's Daniel, a dying young drug addict. Then in 1922, she was seen as an aging actress in Verneuil's *Régine Armand*. The audience cheered when she spoke the lines: "Rest! Do I think of such a thing. Do you believe that I shall ever rest?"

By 1923, she was seriously ill, but the indomitable actress consented to perform the role of a clairvoyant in the motion picture *La Voyante*. It was to be filmed in her home. On March 21, she collapsed and lay dying for several days. Upon hearing that the press was maintaining a 24-hour vigil outside her home, she smilingly said: "The Press has tormented me enough all my life. I can certainly plague it a little by making it [cool] its heels now."[64] Sarah Bernhardt never spoke again and died on March 26 of uremic poisoning. Thousands viewed her body and followed the funeral cortege to the intrepid star's final resting place in the cemetery of Père Lachaise. "Bernhardt" is the sole inscription on her mausoleum.

CHAPTER EIGHT
DUSE 1858-1924

As Adelaide Ristori had contended with Elisa Félix, so Eleonora Duse competed with Sarah Bernhardt. "Eleonora Duse," wrote Bernhardt, "is more a comedian [actress] than an artiste."[1] She claimed that Duse "walks in paths that have been traced out by others....she has never by her art made a single personage stand out identified by her name; she has not created a being or a vision which reminds one of herself."[2] Thus the jealous French tragedienne unwittingly defined her Italian colleague's genius. Duse was a consummate naturalistic actress, while Bernhardt was a brilliant theatrical technician. As Bernhardt strove to heighten her own personality, Duse worked to "forget self."[3]

Unlike the Parisian Sarah Bernhardt, Eleonora Duse grew up in the villages and provincial towns of Northern Italy. She was born on October 3, 1858, in the Cannon d'Oro Inn at Vigevano. Her parents Alessandro and Angelica Duse were mediocre impoverished strolling players, but Alessandro's father Luigi Duse had starred in Venetian comedy. Duse and her parents walked from one village to another with the little girl holding on to her mother's hand and skirt. "I remember Duse," stated the American actress Eva Le Gallienne, "describing to me her arrival in a small town just before dawn. She and her father and the rest of the company had walked all through the night. It was too early to go to the inn, so they washed their hands and faces in the fountain of the public square and sat down to rest on the stone benches, waiting for the day."[4] And the biographer E.A. Rheinhardt wrote:

> To pack up and go on, always to go on, was her first experience of the world. An image of one of those perpetual leave-takings out of the faint dawn of her memory always remained with her. They were staying with kind people; outside it was a rainy winter day; but indoors there were warmth and kindness, and the child had for the first time a sweet and painful sense of home. The good-hearted landlady had given her her first doll, a lovely doll, worthy of all the love of a child. Eleonora never let it out of her arms, slept with it, and was still holding it to her heart when the new leave-taking came. She wept bitterly at first, then she became quiet, grasping the fact that there was no escape from this moving on. The cherished doll was clasped to her breast under her cloak. But after a few steps she tore herself away, ran back to the empty room, laid the doll in the bed where she had slept, and covered it up tenderly. Later she said: "I left it there, so that *it* at least might be warm."[5]

Eleonora Duse made her stage debut at the age of four as Cosette in *Les Misérables*. Later she related that her legs had been switched in the wings, thus adding realism to her tears on stage. Her father taught her to read and write. Undoubtedly he instructed her in acting, which at that time consisted of standardized poses and declamatory speech. The troupe's extensive repertory was composed of Italian adaptations of French tragedies, melodramas, and farces—dramas that Duse eventually condemned as "stupid" and "clumsy." The young actress possessed a fertile imagination. "I used to talk to the chair," Duse said, "or to other objects close at hand, which for me, in their silence, contained a great enchantment—and they seemed to listen patiently to me, who demanded no answer."6

By the age of 12, she was performing leading roles such as Silvio Pellico's Francesca da Rimini and at 14 appeared as Juliet in the Verona arena. Her future lover Gabriele D'Annunzio recalled her description of that evening:

> One Sunday in May, in the immense arena in the amphitheater under the open sky, before an audience that had breathed in the legend of love and death, I was Juliet herself. No thrill from the most responsive audience, no applause, no triumph, ever has had from me the fullness and intoxication of that unique hour. Actually, when I heard Romeo say: 'O, she doth teach the torches to burn bright,' my whole being kindled. With great economy, I had managed to buy a large bunch of roses, and these were my only ornament. I mingled the roses with my words, my gestures, with every attitude. I dropped one at Romeo's feet when we first met; I strewed the petals of another on his head, as I stood on the balcony; and I covered his body with them as he lay in the tomb. The words came with the strangest ease, almost involuntarily, as in delirium, and I could feel the throbbing in my veins accompanying them.
>
> I could see the great amphitheater, half in sunlight, half in shadow, and in the lighter part a sparkling from thousands of eyes. The day was as calm as this. Not a breath of air disturbed the folds of my robes, or the hair that floated on my uncovered neck. I felt my strength and

animation momentarily increasing. How I spoke of the lark and the nightingale! I had heard them both a thousand times in the country. I knew all their songs of the woods, the meadows, and the sky. Every word, as it left my lips, seemed to have been steeped in the warmth of my blood. There was no fiber in me that did not give forth harmonious sound. Ah, the grace, the state of grace! Every time it is given to me to rise to the highest summit of my art I live again in that indescribable *abandon*. Yes, I was Juliet! I cried out in terror at the approach of dawn. The breeze stirred my hair. I could feel the extraordinary silence on which my lamentation fell. The multitude seemed to have sunk into the ground. I spoke of the terror of the coming day, but already I felt in reality 'the mask of night upon my face.' Romeo had descended. We were already dead; already both had entered the vale of shadows....My eyes sought the fading light of the sky. The people were noisy in the arena; they were impatient for the death scene; they would listen no more to the mother, the nurse, or the friar. The quiver of that impatience quickened my throbbing heart. The tragedy swept on. I recall the odor of the pitch from the funeral torches, and of the roses that covered me, and I remember the sound of far-off bells, and of the sky that was losing its light, little by little, as Juliet was losing her life, and a star, the first star, that swam in my eyes with my tears. When I fell dead on Romeo's body, the cry of the multitude in the shadows was so violent that I was frightened. Some one lifted me and dragged me toward that cry. Some one held the torch close to my tear-stained face, which must have been the color of death....And thus...one night in May, Juliet came to life again, and appeared before the people of Verona.7

While in Verona, Duse learned of her mother's death from tuberculosis in a pauper's ward at Ancona. They had left her there when she no longer was able to travel with the company. The young artist could not afford to dress in mourning, but she carried her mother's picture with her until the day she died. Duse also was to suffer from the same disease.

For the next few years, she performed with various companies. Her acting of Ophelia, Vittorio Alfieri's Elettra, and Zola's Thérèse Raquin was noted for restraint and truthfulness.

During a season in Naples, Duse met Martino Cafiero, a cultured and sophisticated newspaper editor. He introduced her to his world of literary intellectuals who both fascinated and stimulated the youthful performer. She always had been an avid reader, especially of actresses' biographies. Her major love affairs were to be with writers. Soon she became Cafiero's mistress and gave birth to his son in 1880. The child died within a few days. Cafiero already had deserted Duse, who was now a member of Cesare Rossi's troupe in Turin.

In May 1880, Eleonora Duse appeared in Dumas *fils' La Princesse de Bagdad*. The play had been a failure in Paris, but Duse's performance was an enormous success. She was praised for "authentic feeling" by Dumas' friend Count Giuseppe Primoli, who wrote the author about his superb new Italian interpreter. The Count and his wealthy, aristocratic acquaintances became Duse's ardent supporters.

Also that year, Duse married Tebaldo Checchi, a character actor who devoted himself to her well-being and career. She bore him a daughter, Enrichetta, in January 1882. The following month, Sarah

Bernhardt and her company arrived in Turin for performances of *La Dame aux Camélias, Adrienne Lecouvreur,* and Henri Meilhac's *Frou-Frou*. Duse attended every performance and stated:

> As a great ship leaves behind it—how do you say it? A wake?—yes, a wake—for a long time the atmosphere of the old theatre remained what she had brought to it. Only she was spoken of in the city, the salons, the theatre. One woman had done that! And, as a reaction, I felt liberated, I felt I had the right to do what I wanted, something other than what was imposed on me....I went every evening to hear her and to weep![8]

Inspired by the French star's example, Duse determined to persist in creating her own distinct style of acting. She declared:

> A part of the public does not yet accept me as I wish to be accepted...because I do things in my own way: I mean, in the way I feel them. It is established that in certain situations the voice must be raised, one must carry on outrageously; and I, on the contrary, when I must express violent passion, when my spirit is gripped by pleasure or sorrow, often fall mute, and on stage I speak softly, barely murmuring....Then certain people say I have no expression, that I do not feel, do not suffer....Ah, but...they will come.[9]

Duse added to her repertoire the role of Dumas' Marguerite Gauthier, one of Sarah Bernhardt's most memorable portrayals. According to the young Italian playwright Luigi Pirandello, Eleonora Duse cast a "romantic spell" enfused with "secret sweetness" and "overwhelming passion."[10] In 1897, the two actresses performed the role concurrently, thus enabling the Parisian public to compare Duse's restrained naturalness to Bernhardt's elegant theatricality.

Duse triumphed, in January 1884, as the tragic Santuzza in Giovanni Verga's realistic play *Cavalleria rusticana*. This was to be one of her most popular roles. The play soon became the libretto for an opera by Pietro Mascagni in which the French singing-actress Emma Calvé caused a sensation at her Metropolitan Opera debut in 1893. Calvé had been inspired by Duse's artistry and wrote:

> I cannot continue the narrative of my years in Italy without speaking of an artist whose influence upon my career has been incalculable—La Duse! All my life, I have loved and admired her deeply. I cannot see her upon the stage without being profoundly moved. Hers was the spark that set my fires alight. Her art, simple, human, passionately sincere, was a revelation to me. It broke down the false and conventional standards of lyric expression to which I had become accustomed. She taught me to appreciate sincerity in art,...I followed her on her tours through Italy one summer, going from town to town where she was playing, attending each performance....[11]

April 1885 saw Duse and the Rossi Company set sail for a tour of South America. She was armed with letters of introduction from the celebrated tragedienne Adelaide Ristori. Despite her gracious gesture, the retired star was critical of the younger artist's acting style. Ristori had been a highly emotional melodramatic performer and said of Duse's naturalness: "Her facial mobility and absence of artificiality are gifts, yet art like hers will die."[12] Duse may have listened politely to Ristori's admonitions, but she was not deterred from pursuing her own artistic course.

Duse's tour of Uruguay, Brazil, and Argentina was a theatrical success, but her marriage foundered. Tired of Tebaldo Checchi, she had an affair with the handsome actor Flavio Ando and returned to Italy intent on forming her own acting troupe. Her husband remained in Argentina as a government official.

Even though her relationship with Ando had ended, Duse still hired the versatile performer as her leading man. Duse both starred in and staged her own productions, consisting mainly of plays by Dumas and Sardou. But this soon was to change because of her association with a new lover, the distinguished opera librettist and composer Arrigo Boito. His vast knowledge and love of literature, ranging from Elizabethan drama to religious mysticism, was to be shared with the receptive young star upon whom it had a lasting effect. Boito's superb libretti for Giuseppi Verdi's *Otello* and later *Falstaff* reflected his lifelong devotion to the works of Shakespeare. He despised the plays of Sardou and Dumas and encouraged Duse to perform in his own translation of Shakespeare's *Antony and Cleopatra*. Boito fervidly supported her artistic individuality. "Do it your own way," he stated, "always in your own way; you will overcome all resistance."[13] The production in November 1888, however, was a failure. Duse forced her voice and resorted to exaggerated gestures. "Shakespeare," she later was to say, "—he is always the God; but, apart from certain sublime creations which I cannot play, I often find in his dramas that the women's parts are sacrificed to the men's."[14] Although she never assayed another Shakespearean role, Duse remained a devotee of his writings, reading them in French translation. But a friend recalled:

> She loved to hear the sound of Shakespeare's own words, and would ask me to read it aloud to her. Then she would sit awhile pondering over it in silence. 'The sound reflects the meaning,' she would say; 'blood; drowsy; incarnadine; those words *sound* like their meaning.' Then, after a moment, she added: 'Of course it is Macbeth himself one would want to play. What an extraordinary, complex nature! In spite of his maleness—so much *woman* in him! Ah, Shakespeare! He knew everything!'[15]

Duse and Boito shared a jealously guarded need for privacy in both their work and lives. "The one happiness," exclaimed the actress, "is to shut one's door upon a little room, with a table before one, and to create; to create life in that isolation from life."[16] The biographer Arthur Symons described Duse's creative process as follows:

> She began by learning her parts by heart; then in one of her rooms, where she had absolute quiet, in Rome, London, Venice or elsewhere, she would fling the window wide open, put her feet on a chair, lean back in an armchair, the play-book on her knees, which she rarely opened, drinking in as one drinks wine the scented air, and all the time, her imagination wide awake, the character she had to represent would loom up before her; and she would seize on this one character until feature by feature, gesture by gesture, movement by movement, it revealed itself to her by the inevitable slow process of Nature herself in the act of

creation. This would go on for days and weeks; when any idea struck her, in regard to some phrase, some interpretation, she would make rapid notes in the margin with her pencil; which means a slow and laborious but certain manner of achieving an end.[17]

Unlike Sarah Bernhardt who fostered publicity, Eleonora Duse resented any invasion of her private life by either the public or the press. "Let them come and see my work,"[18] she stated, and preferably the "cultured, educated and impartial."[19]

During 1890 and 1891, Duse took her company to Egypt, Spain, and Russia. While in St. Petersburg, she was seen by the young playwright Anton Chekhov, who wrote:

> I have just seen the Italian actress Duse in Shakespeare's *Cleopatra*. I do not know Italian, but she acted so well that I felt I was understanding every word. What a marvelous actress! Never before have I seen anything like it. I looked at this Duse and I felt sadness, because we must educate our sensibilities and our tastes through wooden actresses like X—and the others who resemble her, and that we consider great because we have seen no better. As I was watching la Duse, I realized why we are bored in the Russian theatre....[20]

The Russian press concurred, praising the artist for her naturalness. "She does not gesticulate," wrote the critic Alexey Suvorin, "does not declaim, does not invent scenic effects, but creates characters, lives them with a simplicity never seen before on the stage."[21]

The year 1891 was significant for the Italian star. Aside from her artistic acclaim in Russia, Eleonora Duse appeared for the first time as Nora in Ibsen's *A Doll's House*. The play not only featured Duse's initial portrayal of an Ibsen character but was the first Italian production of a drama by the Norwegian playwright. Duse was to become one of Ibsen's major advocates and interpreters.

The actress' success in Russia was repeated the following year in Austria. Like Chekhov in St. Petersburg, Hugo von Hofmannstahl in Vienna admired Duse's psychological motivation of character. This was echoed in Berlin by Gerhart Hauptmann, who regarded her as the greatest exponent of the new "psychological art."

Following her European victories, Duse launched forth in early 1893 for New York. She opened on January 23 as Dumas' Marguerite Gauthier. "I suspect that Eleonora Duse is the greatest actress in the world,"[22] claimed the noted American performer Mrs. Minnie Maddern Fiske. The naturalness of Duse's acting was a new experience to many of her viewers. Her entrances were unobtrusive, and occasionally she performed with her back to the public. In addition, she refused to be interviewed. Duse did, however, write a letter to the press explaining her need for privacy: "I am especially the slave of my temperament which does not allow me, alas, simply to 'play' my parts but, much against my will, forces me to suffer with the beings I am forced to represent."[23]

Duse's stage direction also was commended. She was an assiduously methodical director. "My poor prose," wrote the playwright Marco Praga of his work *La moglie ideale*, "spoken like that, as la Duse spoke it, and as she made her actors speak, and she commented on it and explained it, and illustrated it to train her colleagues, to give them the right tones, the right gestures, the necessary movements."[24]

Her New York engagement was followed by performances in Philadelphia, Chicago, and Boston. Then on April 22, she and her company left for England and appearances at London's Lyric Theatre. After engagements in Vienna, Berlin, and Munich, she disbanded her company on January 31, 1894.

In spring of 1894, she joined Cesare Rossi's troupe for a season in London, including a special performance for Queen Victoria at Windsor Castle. Duse was frustrated, however, by the troupe's inadequacy and again formed her own company a few months later. In early 1895, the actress-manager began a tour of Holland, Belgium, and Germany, culminating in a season at London's Theatre Royal, Drury Lane. The English critic and playwright George Bernard Shaw wrote:

> I should say without qualification that it is the best modern acting I have ever seen....There are years of work, bodily and mental, behind every instant of it—work, mind, not mere practice and habit, which is quite a different thing. It is the rarity of the gigantic energy needed to sustain this work which makes Duse so exceptional; for the work is in her case highly intellectual work, and so requires energy of a quality altogether superior to the mere head of steam needed to produce Bernhardtian explosions with the requisite regularity.[25]

Sarah Bernhardt was appearing at Daly's Theatre in London, and Shaw compared the two artists' performances of Magda in Hermann Sudermann's *Heimat*:

> Those charming roseate effects which French painters

produce by giving flesh the pretty color of strawberries and cream, and painting the shadows pink and crimson are cunningly reproduced by Madame Bernhardt in the living picture. She paints her ears crimson and allows them to peep enchantingly through a few loose braids of her auburn hair. Every dimple has its dab of pink; and her finger-tips are so delicately incarnadined that you fancy they are transparent like her ears, and that the light is shining through their delicate blood-vessels. Her lips are like a newly painted pillar box; her cheeks, right up to the languid lashes, have the bloom and surface of a peach; she is beautiful with the beauty of her school, and entirely inhuman and incredible....And it is always Sarah Bernhardt in her own capacity who does this to you. The dress, the title of the play, the order of the words may vary; but the woman is always the same. She does not enter into the leading character; she substitutes herself for it.

All this is precisely what does not happen in the case of Duse, whose every part is a separate creation. When she comes on the stage, you are quite welcome to take your opera-glass and count whatever lines time and care have so far traced on her. They are the credentials of her humanity; and she knows better than to obliterate that significant handwriting beneath a layer of peach-bloom from the chemist's. The shadows on her face are gray, not crimson; her lips are sometimes nearly gray also; there are neither dabs nor dimples....When it is remembered that the majority of tragic actors excel only in explosions of those passions which are common to man and brute, there will be no difficulty in understanding the indescribable distinction which Duse's acting acquires from the fact that behind every stroke of it is a distinctively human idea....

Obvious as the disparity of the two famous artists has been to many of us since we first saw Duse, I doubt whether any of us realized, after Madame Bernhardt's very clever performance as Magda on Monday night, that there was room in the nature of things for its annihilation within forty-eight hours by so comparatively quiet a talent as Duse's. And yet annihilation is the only word for it. Sarah was very charming, very jolly when the sun shone, very petulant when the clouds covered it, and positively angry when they wanted to take her child away from her. And she did not trouble us with any fuss about the main theme of Sudermann's play, the revolt of the modern woman against that ideal of home which exacts the sacrifice of her whole life to its care, not by her grace, and as its own sole help and refuge, but as a right which it has to the services of the females as abject slaves. In fact, there is not the slightest reason to suspect Madame Bernhardt of having discovered any such theme in the play; though Duse, with one look at Schwartze, the father, nailed it to the stage as the subject of the impending dramatic struggle before she had been five minutes on the scene. Before long, there came a stroke of acting which will probably never be forgotten by those who saw it, and which explained at once why those artifices of the dressing-table which help Madame Bernhardt would hinder Duse almost as much as a screen placed in front of her. I should explain, first, that the real name of the play is not "Magda" but "Home." Magda is a daughter who has been turned out of doors for defying her father, one of those outrageous persons who mistake their desire to have everything their own way in the house for a sacred principle of home life. She has a hard time of it, but at last makes a success as an opera singer, though not until her lonely struggles have thrown her for sympathy on a fellow student, who in due time goes his way, and leaves her to face motherhood as best she can. In the fullness of her fame she returns to her native town, and in an attack of homesickness makes advances to her father, who consents to receive her again. No sooner is she installed in the house than she finds that one of the most intimate friends of the family is the father of her child. In the third act of the play she is on the stage when he is announced as a visitor. It must be admitted that Sarah Bernhardt played this scene very lightly and pleasantly: there was genuine good fellowship in the way in which she reassured the embarrassed gallant and made him understand that she was not going to play off the sorrows of Gretchen on him after all those years, and that she felt that she owed him the priceless experience of maternity, even if she did not particularly respect him for it. Her self-possession at this point was immense: the peach-bloom never altered by a shade. Not so with Duse. The moment she read the card handed her by the servant, you realized what it was to have to face a meeting with the man. It was interesting to watch how she got through it when he came in, and how, on the whole, she got through it pretty well. He paid his compliments and offered his flowers; they sat down; and she evidently felt that she had got it safely over and might allow herself to think at her ease, and to look at him to see how much he had altered. Then a terrible thing happened to her. She began to blush; and in another moment she was conscious of it, and the blush was slowly spreading and deepening until, after a few vain efforts to avert her face or to obstruct his view of it without seeming to do so, she gave up and hid the blush in her hands. After that feat of acting I did not need to be told why Duse does not paint an inch thick. I could detect no trick in it: it seemed to me a perfectly genuine effect of the dramatic imagination.[26]

Following her London triumphs, Eleonora Duse returned to Italy. Her affair with Arrigo Boito had ended and she fell passionately in love with the noted poet and womanizer Gabriele D'Annunzio. Duse was bored with her present repertory, referring to the heroine of Dumas' *La Dame aux Camélias* as "That stupid woman." D'Annunzio offered to write verse dramas for her. His conception of the drama as "a revelation of beauty" and "an ideal transfiguration of life"[27] appealed to the visionary actress. Both contemplated the creation of a Bayreuthesque festival theatre near Rome in which to perform these works.

Duse returned to the United States on February 6, 1896. The reviews in New York, Philadelphia, Boston, and Washington were glowing. Mrs. Grover Cleveland invited the actress to tea at the White House, and Thomas Edison recorded her voice at his Menlo Park Studio in New Jersey.

The Italian star had avoided performances in Paris, the bastion of Sarah Bernhardt. But in 1897, she was invited by the French artist to appear at her own theatre the Renaissance. Duse made her Parisian debut as Marguerite Gauthier. She often opened a new season with this role, and it was Bernhardt's tour de force. Present in the audience were the actresses Sarah Bernhardt and Réjane, the diseuse Yvette Guilbert, the critic Francisque Sarcey, and the aristocracy of France. Duse was nervous, and the reviews were reserved. There was more approbation for her portrayal of Sudermann's Magda and unmitigated praise for her performance in Dumas *fils' La Femme de Claude*. In addition, she appeared in the world premiere of D'Annunzio's morbid Renaissance play, *Il sogno d'un mattino di primavera*. Upon the suggestion of Sarcey, Duse presented a professional matinee for the French actors and actresses who had been unable to attend her performances. She was seen in *Cavalleria rusticana*, the fifth act of *La Dame aux Camélias*, and the second act of *La Femme de Claude*. The matinee took place in the Théâtre de la Porte Saint-Martin because Bernhardt spitefully refused a one-day extension on Duse's lease at the Renaissance. "She has won us," stated Sarcey, "by the sheer power of truth."[28] For the remainder of their careers, Bernhardt jealously criticized her Italian colleague, while Duse continued to speak well of the French star.

During the next two years, Duse performed in Venice, Milan, Rome, Naples, Monte Carlo, Marseilles, Lisbon, Genoa, Bologna, Cairo, and Athens. Large sums of money were needed to support D'Annunzio's extravagances. By 1899, he had completed the plays *La Gioconda* and *La gloria* in which Duse starred. *La gloria* was a failure, but *La Gioconda* gradually gained acceptance.

Duse's love affair with D'Annunzio was turbulent. She was deeply distressed by the poet's numerous infidelities and by the graphic depiction of their relationship in his novel *Il fuoco* which portrayed her as an aging actress, desperately in love with a youthful poet. Her friends and public were scandalized at the book's publication in 1900. Duse, however, refrained from comment except in private reproaches to D'Annunzio. Her faith in his artistic genius never wavered.

La Gioconda had become part of her standard repertory. She added D'Annunzio's *La citta morta* and *Francesca da Rimini* in 1901. Many advised the actress against performing these morbid, elaborately verbose, historical verse dramas. But she remained adamant in support of his works. Even during her tour of the United States in 1902, she insisted upon a repertory of D'Annunzio's plays. They proved generally unpopular with the critics and audiences. James Huneker of the *New York Sun*, however, was later to write of Duse's performance in *La Gioconda*: "Throughout this most human among actresses is in constant modulation; her very silence is pregnant with suggestion. She is the exponent of an art that is baffling in its coincidence with nature."[29] This same naturalism was noted by Ellen Terry who recalled: "But it is as the real woman, a particular woman, that Duse triumphs most."[30] And of the emotionally charged silences, Eva Le Gallienne was to write:

> I have never seen any other actress with such repose. Sometimes she would sit in a chair for a long period completely motionless, holding us all spellbound by sheer intensity of thought. She did not need physical motion, not even facial expression, to convey her thoughts; she conveyed them because she *really* thought them—she did not merely pretend to think them.[31]

Duse returned to Europe and soon commenced preparations for

D'Annunzio's new tragedy *La figlia di Jorio*. Shortly before the opening, however, she was taken ill and requested a delay. D'Annunzio refused, and Duse withdrew from the production. Her replacement, Irma Gramatica, triumphed in the poet's one genuinely successful play. The lovers parted, terminating their ten-year artistic and personal relationship.

After her break with D'Annunzio, Duse dropped all of his plays except *La Gioconda* from her repertory. She returned to Dumas' *La Dame aux Camélias*, Scribe's *Adrienne Lecouvreur*, Pinero's *The Second Mrs. Tanqueray*, Sudermann's *Heimat*, and Ibsen's two works *A Doll's House* and *Hedda Gabler*. Later she added the Scandinavian playwright's *John Gabriel Borkman*, *The Lady for the Sea*, and *Rosmersholm*. The latter production was designed by the innovative theatre artist Gordon Craig. In addition, she appeared as Wassilissa in a benefit performance of Maxim Gorky's *The Lower Depths* at Aurélien-Marie Lugné-Poë's Nouveau Théâtre in Paris. For five years, her tours included performances in Europe, Scandinavia, South America, and Russia. Then, to the astonishment of the theatre world, Eleonora Duse dissolved her company and ceased acting at the end of January 1909.

Duse long had been disenchanted with her profession. "Those cursed boards!" she would exclaim. The actress had been on the stage since the age of four. Often Duse had performed roles for which she felt only contempt. "Out of the two hundred plays I have performed," she said, "there are hardly ten that I love." Amongst these were the plays of Ibsen. "Ibsen," she stated, "yes, Ibsen, and always nothing but Ibsen."[32] So great was Duse's admiration for his works that when performing in Kristiania, Norway, "she waited...on the sidewalk, opposite his home, ...awaiting the silhouette of the old poet behind the large window."[33] But above all, Duse yearned for that "inner harmony" urged upon her by Boito.

"Don't you know," she once cried to a friend, "that there are a thousand women in me, and that I am tormented by each one in turn?"[34]

During the next 11 years, Eleonora Duse did not appear on the stage. Instead, she visited friends, established an unsuccessful Actresses' Library for "the intellectual education of poor actresses,"[35] and devoted countless hours to reading. Of special interest to her were books on philosophy and religion. These included the writings of St. Thomas Aquinas, St. Augustine, and various Oriental mystics.

But in 1914, Duse became fascinated with moving pictures and studied them closely. "If I were twenty years younger," she was to remark, "I would begin all over again on the films."[36] She went on to say:

> I am certain that I could do a great deal on them and perhaps evolve something like a completely new form of art. Of course, that would mean creating a new technique: one would have to forget the theatre entirely and learn how to express oneself in the language of the films, which is as yet undeveloped. I made the same mistake as nearly everybody has made: in spite of myself I acted as if I were on the stage. But something quite different is needed; a new and more effective kind of poetry, a new expression of the human soul....I am too old for it, isn't it a pity?[37]

Various Italian film directors and D. W. Griffith in Hollywood offered her contracts. Finally she chose Arturo Ambrosio to produce a motion picture for her entitled *Cenere* [Ashes], based upon a novel by Grazia Deledda. Duse regarded films as animated illustrations. "This is a book I am going to 'illustrate,'" she wrote to her daughter, the wife of a Cambridge University professor. She was intrigued by the films' unlimited opportunities for intricate use of mime. "There are here," she added, "some pages of reality and poetry, which assail my heart and imagination, and which, I believe, without speaking, I will be able to make people understand."[38] Duse performed without uttering a word. "My mouth remains shut;" she related, "a yes or no with the head - and there are some very sad nos."[39] The film received little notice. The simplicity and naturalness of her acting were ahead of their time. "They reproach me," she said, "for the poverty of the story. Did they expect me to play Lady Macbeth or Cleopatra?...As if everything didn't come down finally to a handful of ashes."[40]

Duse wished to follow *Cenere* with a film on the life of Angela da Foligno, a medieval saint, but she was unable to find a producer. "No use thinking of interesting subjects;" she complained, "They don't want art or soul or good work. Some trivial story with a happy ending satisfies them....What they want are young and beautiful women prepared to perform any gymnastics, that's all. There's no place for Angela da Foligno, still less for me...."[41]

During the First World War, Duse devoted much time to aiding the wounded. She wrote letters for them and delivered messages to loved ones. In addition, she shared her income and possessions with the war's refugees. This income, however, soon disappeared. Duse's earnings had been invested by her friend Robert von Mendelssohn in his family's Berlin bank, and postwar inflation obliterated these funds. She was forced to resume her stage career although her fragile health had deteriorated significantly during the war years.

On May 5, 1921, at Turin's Teatro Balbo, Duse returned to the stage with Ermete Zacconi's company in Ibsen's *The Lady from the Sea*. The public and press were united in their praise of her acting. "The great success of the first night in Turin at the hour of return!" she recalled,

"Indeed, everyone was moved. I alone was not. This success belonged to something much greater than I, it passed over my head, it was directed to a force which I represented, but which was not I."[42] Duse's religious concepts permeated her art. "Whenever she gave a superlatively great performance," wrote Eva Le Gallienne, "she never felt that *she* had given it, but rather that it "had been given her" to give—"à moi indigne." At those times when she reached "the summit of her art" it was like an answer to a prayer; and the prayer was never "let me play well for my own sake," but rather simply "let me serve, for the greater glory of God!""[43]

Eleonora Duse next appeared in Marco Praga's *La porta chiusa*. Soon the actress formed her own company for a tour of Italy, concluding with performances in Rome, where she was acclaimed for her portrayal of Mrs. Alving in Ibsen's *Ghosts*.

After a period of rest, she accepted an offer from the English producer C. B. Cochran to give six performances in London during June 1923. Duse received excellent reviews and played to sold-out houses.

Following performances in Vienna, the Italian star sailed for a tour of the United States. On October 29, 1923, she appeared as Ellida in *The Lady from the Sea* at New York's Metropolitan Opera House. "The day before her opening," recorded Miss Le Gallienne, "I went to see her, and found her sitting in her bedroom, on a straight chair facing into a corner of the room. She got up when I came in and explained that she had been sitting like that for several hours, *'en prière,'* she said, *'Je tâche de m'oublier - de me libérer de moi-même....Ainsi j'aurai peut-être moins peur.'*" [in prayer,...I am trying to forget myself - to free myself from myself....Thus, perhaps I shall be less afraid.][44] Duse's performance was well received as were succeeding ones at the new Century Theater. Eva Le Gallienne said of her acting:

> The things that startled and amazed me most in Duse's work were its originality, its boldness, and its truth. I had never before seen technical virtuosity so perfectly concealed. Madame Sarah was a great technician, but one was always aware of her technique. She filled the theatre with excitement, but it was theatrical excitement, not the excitement of life itself. Compared with Duse's, her art was overstressed, overdecorated, overactive. With Duse, one thought of Rimbaud's saying: "Action is a way of spoiling something." She had worked to eliminate everything that was non-essential. Everything she did seemed inevitable. Her art was simple, economical, stripped. When Bernhardt acted you knew she was doing something extremely difficult superlatively well. With Duse you were not aware that she was "doing" anything: it was so effortless; it seemed so easy; no wonder so many people failed to realize the immense discipline behind it all. Yet with this ease, this seeming indifference to effect, Duse had a power that subdued an audience in a way which even Bernhardt's fireworks failed to do. Never have I known such silence in an audience. There was literally not a sound in those vast, crowded houses.[45]

Miss Le Gallienne wrote a fascinating description of Duse's performance in *la città morta* contrasted with Bernhardt's portrayal of the same work:

> The final moments of *La Città Morta* were another example of the amazing power and boldness of Duse's

stillness. Helen Lohman told me of seeing Sarah Bernhardt in the part of the blind woman, Anna, in this play. Sarah—as probably most actresses would have done—closely followed d'Annunzio's very theatrical stage directions: "Anna has felt the lifeless body against her feet. She stoops over the dead girl, utterly distracted, feeling about until she reaches the face and hair, still wet with the death-giving water. She shudders from head to foot, then utters a piercing shriek in which she seems to exhale her soul, and cries: 'I see! I see!'" When Anna recovered her sight, Sarah gave the "shriek," and screamed *"Je vois! Je vois!"* in a loud voice.

When Duse discovered the dead girl, and through the shock, regained her sight, her eyes, which—though open throughout the play—had seemed dead, slowly became alive. One *saw* her see for the first time. For several moments she was completely still, until the realization that she was actually able to see slowly penetrated her consciousness. Then she gave a cry—not a "piercing shriek"—which truly seemed to be the exhalation of her soul, so full was it of wonder at seeing, of horror at what she saw, and mingled joy and anguish at the gift of sight coming to her at such a price. Then, in a very low voice, she said the words, as though scarcely believing what she said: "Vedo! Vedo!"[46]

After the performances in New York, Duse and her company travelled to Baltimore, Philadelphia, Washington, Boston, Chicago, New

Orleans, Havana, Los Angeles, San Francisco, Detroit, Indianapolis, and Pittsburgh. In Los Angeles, she was seen by Charles Chaplin who recorded: "Bernhardt was always studied and more or less artificial. Duse is direct and terrible." He referred to her as "the perfect artist" possessing "the simple, direct child soul; the experienced craftsman in technique; the heart that has been taught the lesson of human sympathy, and the incisive analytical brain of the psychologist." Then he movingly described her performance as the mother in *La porta chiusa* discovering her son's knowledge of his illegitimacy:

> An actress of lesser genius would have torn this emotion absolutely to tatters. Duse sank into a chair and curled up her body almost like a little child in pain. You did not see her face, there was no heaving of the shoulders. She lay quietly almost without moving. Only once through her body ran a sort of shudder of pain like a paroxysm. That and the instinctive shrinking of her body from her son's outstretched hand were almost the only visible movement. Yet so great is her dramatic power, so tremendous is her knowledge of dramatic technique, that this scene fairly wrung your heart. I confess it drew tears from me....When she turned at last, both hands flung out in one gesture of utter despair, resignation—surrender—it was the finest thing I have seen on the stage. Through all her grief, her self-abasement, her contrition, ran terrible irony. It was all in that one gesture.[47]

By the time she arrived in Pittsburgh, Eleonora Duse was exhausted. She opened on April 5, 1924, in *la porta chiusa*. "Duse always arrived at the theatre," related Miss Le Gallienne, "far ahead of time. The stage door—in no way different from the rest—was on the far side of the building, and by the time they at last discovered it they were both drenched, and Duse was chilled through and through."[48] Following the performance, she returned to her hotel gravely ill and for two weeks struggled against pneumonia. "We must move!" cried out the feverish artist on April 21, 1924, and then passed away. After services in Pittsburgh, New York, and Rome, Duse's body was laid to rest in the cemetery of Sant' Anna at her home in Asolo.

NOTES

Chapter One

1Procopius, *Anecdota* (London: William Heinemann, Ltd., MCMXXXV), p. 109.

Chapter Two

1Morris Bishop, trans., *Eight Plays by Molière* (New York: The Modern Library, 1957), p. 132.

2Bishop, p. 132.

3"Il n'y a plus de Desoeillets." *Galerie théâtrale* (Paris: Bance aîné, 1812-1834), planche soixante-seizième, p. 2.

4"*Ris donc, sot de parterre, ris donc a l'endroit le plus touchant de la pièce.*" *Ibid, planche quatre-vingt-quatrième*, p.2.

5Jack Richtman. *Adrienne Lecouvreur The Actress and the Age.* Englewood Cliffs, NJ: Prentice Hall, Inc., 1971, pp. 99-102.

6Jean Racine, *Complete Plays*, trans. S. Solomon (New York: Random House, 1967), p. 272.

7Voltaire, *Candide and Other Stories*, trans. J. Spencer (London: Oxford University Press, 1966), p. 183.

8Frederick Hawkins, *The French Stage in the Eighteenth Century* (New York: Haskell House Publishers Ltd., 1969), I, p. 354.

9T. Cole and H.K. Chinoy, *Actors on Acting* (New York: Crown Publishers, 1970), p. 175.

10Denise Diderot, *Paradox of Acting*, trans. W.H. Pollock (New York: Hill and Wang, 1957), p. 17.

11Hippolyte Clairon, *Memoirs of Hippolyte Clairon* (London: G.G. and J. Robinson, 1800), p. 34.

12*Ibid*, p. 32.

13*Ibid*, p. 35.

14David Garrick, *The Letters of David Garrick*, ed. D.M. Little and G.M. Kahrl (Cambridge, MA: Harvard University Press, 1963), II, p. 635.

15"Il faut dans tous mes rôles que le costume soit observé: la vérité de la déclamation tient à celle du vêtement." Jean Francois Marmontel, *Oeuvres complètes de Marmontel. Tome Premier: Mémoires* (Paris: Chez Verdiere, Libraire - Editeur, 1818), I, p. 298.

16Gerda Taranow, *Sarah Bernhardt* (Princeton: Princeton University Press, 1972), P. 184.

17James Agate, *Rachel* (New York: Viking Press, 1928), p. 28.

Chapter Three

1P. Fitzgerald, *A New History of the English Stage* (London: Tinsley Brothers, 1882), I, p. 80.

2Colley Cibber, *An Apology for the Life of Mr. Colley Cibber* (London: John C. Nimmo, 1889), I, pp. 161-62.

3Helen McAfee, *Pepys on the Restoration Stage* (New York: Benjamin Blom, Inc.), p. 244.

[4]John Dryden, *The Dramatic Works of John Dryden*, ed. G. Saintsbury (Edinburgh, Scotland: William Paterson, 1882), III, p. 468.

[5]McAfee, p. 247.

[6]J.P. Kenyon, *The Stuarts* (London: Severn House, 1977), p. 134.

[7]P.H. Highfill, Jr., K.A. Burnim, E.A. Langhans, eds., *A Biographical Dictionary of Actors, Actresses, Musicians, Dancers, Managers and Other Stage Personnel in London, 1660-1800*. (Carbondale and Edwardsville, IL: Southern Illinois University Press, 1973), I, 314.

[8]Charles Gildon, *The Life of Mr. Thomas Betterton* (London: Robert Gosling, 1710), p. 16.

[9]*Ibid*, p. 40.

[10]Cibber, I, p. 160.

[11]Scott McMillin, ed., *Restoration and Eighteenth Century Comedy* (New York: W.W. Norton & Company, Inc., 1973), p. 173.

[12]Highfill, II, p. 280.

[13]Cibber, I, p. 307.

[14]*Ibid*, II, pp. 70-71.

[15]T. Chetwood, *A General History of the Stage* (London: W. Owen, 1749), p. 201.

[16]Cibber, I, p. 310.

[17]*Ibid.*, I, p. 51.

[18]Richard Steele, *The Tatler* (Philadelphia: J.J. Woodward, 1831), p. 358.

[19]Cibber, I, p. 309.

[20]Thomas Davies, *Memoirs of the Life of David Garrick, Esq.* (New York: Benjamin Blom, Inc., 1969), II, p. 189.

[21]John Hill, *The Actor Or, A Treatise on the Art of Playing* (New York: Benjamin Blom, Inc., 1972), p. 60.

[22]James Boswell, *Life of Johnson* (New York: Everyman Edition), II, pp. 484-85.

[23]Thomas Gray, *Correspondence of Thomas Gray*, eds. Paget Toynbee and Leonard Whibley (Oxford: The Clarendon Press, 1935), II, p. 778.

[24]Bertram Joseph, *The Tragic Actor* (London: Routledge and Kegan Paul, 1959), p. 160.

[25]Tate Wilkinson, *Memoirs of his own Life* (York, England: Wilson, Spence and Mawman, 1790), p. 34.

[26]Janet Dunbar, *Peg Woffington and Her World* (Boston: Houghton Mifflin Company, 1968), p. 92.

[27]Chetwood, p. 252.

[28]Wilkinson, pp. 118-19.

[29]Thomas Campbell, *Life of Mrs. Siddons* (London: Effingham Wilson, 1834), II, pp. 35-36.

[30]Ibid., pp. 10-34.

[31]W.C. Macready, *Macready's Reminiscences*, ed. Frederick Pollock (New York: MacMillan and Co., 1875), p. 44.

[32]Campbell, I, p. 75.

33Hester Lynch Thrale Piozzi, *Thraliana: The Diary of Mrs. Hester Lynch Thrale*, ed. K.C. Balderston (London: Oxford at the Clarendon Press, 1951), vol. 2, p. 715.

34Macready, pp. 42-43.

35Campbell, pp. 37-39.

36Mrs. Clement Parsons, *The Incomparable Siddons* (London: Methuen & Co., 1909), p. 75.

37Campbell, I, pp. 215-16.

38*Ibid.*, I, p. 237.

39A.C. Sprague, *Shakespearian Players and Performances* (Cambridge, MA: Harvard University Press, 1953), p. 69.

40P.W. Clayden, *Rogers and his Contemporaries* (London: Smith, Elder & Co., 1889), I, p. 354.

Chapter Four

1Frances Ann Kemble, *Records of a Girlhood*, 2nd ed. (New York: Henry Holt and Company, 1884), p. 15.

2Joseph N. Ireland, *Records of the New York Stage from 1750-1860*, 2 vols (New York: T.H. Morrell, 1866-67), p. 21.

3Hugh F. Rankin, *The Theatre in Colonial America* (Chapel Hill, NC: University of North Carolina Press, 1960), p. 65.

4Alexander Graydon, *Memoirs of a Life Chiefly Passed in Pennsylvania within the Last Sixty YEars* (Harrisburg: 1811), p. 76.

5William Dunlap, *History of the American Theatre*, vol. 1 (New York: J. and J. Harper, 1832), p. 40.

[6]George O. Seilhamer, *History of the American Theatre*, vol. I (Philadelphia: Globe Printing House, 1888), p. 339.

[7]Dunlap, vol. 1, p. 335.

[8]*Ibid.*, pp. 336-7.

[9]Ireland, p. 155.

[10]*Ibid.*

[11]*Ibid.*

[12]George C. Odell, *Annals of the New York Stage*, vol. II (New York: Columbia University Press, 1927-49), p. 120.

[13]*Ibid.*, p. 135.

[14]Dunlap, p. 334.

[15]*Ibid.*, p. 308.

[16]Ireland, p. 155.

[17]*Ibid.*, p. 11.

[18]*Ibid.*, p. 17.

[19]*Ibid.*, p. 45.

[20]*Ibid.*, p. 22.

[21]*Ibid.*, p. 26-7.

[22]*Ibid.*, p. 29.

[23]*Ibid.*

[24]*Ibid.*, p. 33.

[25]*Ibid.*, p. 40.

[26]Horace Greeley, *Recollections of a Busy Life* (New York: J.B. Ford and Company, 1868), p. 203.

[27]Ireland, p. 117.

[28]*Ibid.*, pp. 80-2.

[29]*Ibid.*, p. 3.

[30]*Ibid.*, p. 140.

[31]Emma Stebbins, ed., *Charlotte Cushman: Her Letters and Memories of Her Life* (Boston: Houghton, Osgood and Company, 1878), p. 16.

[32]*Ibid.*, p. 22.

[33]H. Barton Baker, *The London Stage: Its History and Traditions from 1576 to 1888*, vol. II (London: W.H. Allen and Co., 1889), p. 163.

[34]William Winter, *Other Days* (New York: Moffat, Yard & Co., 1908), pp. 152-3.

[35]George Vandenhoff, *Leaves from an Actor's Note-Book, or Anecdotes of the Green-Room and Stage at Home and Abroad* (London: T.W. Cooper and Company, 1860), p. 184.

[36]Eleanor Ruggles, *Prince of Players* (New York: W.W. Norton and Company, Inc., 1953), p. 116.

[37]*Cincinnati Commercial*, March 4, 1875, p. 12.

[38]Garff B. Wilson, *A History of American Acting* (Bloomington, IN: Indiana University Press, 1966), p. 50.

[39]Vandenhoff, pp. 183-4.

[40]Clara Erskine Clement, *Charlotte Cushman*. American Actor Series. Ed. by Laurence Hutton (Boston: James R. Osgood and Company, 1882), p. 25.

[41]Mary Anderson, *A Few Memories* (New York: Harper and Brothers, 1896), p. 38.

[42]Lawrence Barrett, *Charlotte Cushman: A Lecture by Lawrence Barrett* (New York: The Dunlap Society, 1889), p. 14.

[43]Stebbins, pp. 263-4.

[44]Barrett, p. 17.

[45]Arthur and Barbara Gelb, *O'Neill* (New York: Harper, 1962), p. 25.

[46]Wilson, p. 51.

[47]Stebbins, p. 24.

[48]Stebbins, p. 55.

[49]Kate Louise Roberts, ed., *Hoyt's New Cyclopedia of Practical Quotations* (New York: Funk & Wagnalls Co., 1940), p. 4.

[50]Winter, *Other Days*, p. 153.

[51]Stebbins, p. 238.

[52]William Winter, *The Wallet of Time* (New York: Moffat, Yard & Co., 1913), p. 159.

Chapter Five

[1] Lloyd Morris, *Curtain Time: The Story of the American Theater* (New York: Random House, 1953), p. 117.

[2] Bernard Falk, *Rachel the Immoral* (New York: Benjamin Blom, Inc., 1972), p. 232.

[3] Mrs. Arthur Kennard, *Rachel* (London: Witt, Allen & Co., 1885), p. 9.

[4] *Ibid.*, p. 22.

[5] *Ibid.*, p. 19.

[6] Falk, p. 37.

[7] *Ibid.*, p. 217.

[8] Kennard, p. 92.

[9] James Agate, *Rachel* (New York: The Viking Press, 1928), p. 134.

[10] Joanna Richardson, *Rachel* (London: Max Reinhardt, 1956), p. 47.

[11] *Ibid.*, p. 37.

[12] Falk, p. 302.

[13] Kennard, p. 28.

[14] *Ibid.*, pp. 33-4.

[15] *Ibid.*, p. 92.

[16] Falk, p. 259.

[17] Agate, p. 42.

[18] Falk, p. 148.

[19] Kennard, p. 72 (*"Ah, je suis fatiguée. J'ai besoin de m'encanailler."*)

[20] *Ibid.*, p. 112.

[21] *The London Times*, May 11, 1841, p. 5.

[22] Fanny Kemble, *Records of Later Life* (New York: Henry Holt and Company, 1884), pp. 244-5.

[23] *Ibid.*, p. 245.

[24] *Ibid.*

[25] Charlotte Brontë, *Villette*, vol. II (London: J.M. Dent and Company, MDCCCXCIII), pp. 11-12.

[26] Kennard, p. 131.

[27] *Ibid.*, p. 132.

[28] Richardson, p. 59.

[29] Falk, p. 137.

[30] George Henry Lewes, *Dramatic Essays* (London: Walter Scott, Limited, 1896), pp. 84-5.

[31] Kennard, p. 132.

[32] Falk, p. 146.

[33] Agate, p. 68 (*"Quelle route! Quelle fatique! ma quelle dot!"*).

[34] H. Sutherland Edwards, *Idols of the French Stage*, vol. II (London: Remington & Co., Publishers, 1899), pp. 267-9.

[35]Kemble, p. 246.

[36]Kennard, p. 177.

[37]*Ibid.*

[38]Richardson, p. 112.

[39]*Ibid.* p. 96.

[40]Kennard, p. 143.

[41]Richardson, p. 96.

[42]Kennard, p. 143.

[43]*Ibid.*, pp. 182-3.

[44]Adelaide Ristori, *Memoirs and Artistic Studies* (New York: Benjamin Blom, 1969), p. 31.

[45]*Ibid.*, p. 35.

[46]*Ibid.*

[47]Henry Morley, *The Journal of a London Playgoer* (London: George Routledge and Sons, Limited, 1891), p. 174.

[48]Ristori, p. 220.

[49]Richardson, p. 157.

[50]Odell, vol. VI, p. 448.

[51]"The Editor's Easy Chair," *Harpers Magazine,* November, 1855, p. 843.

[52]Léon Beauvallet, *Rachel and the New World* (New York: Abelard-Schuman Limited, 1967), p. 62.

[53]*Ibid.*, p. 64.

[54]*Ibid.*

[55]Kennard, p. 220.

[56]Richardson, p. 71.

[57]Kennard, p. 220.

[58]Falk, p. 302.

[59]Lewes, p. 98.

[60]Kemble, p. 246.

Chapter Six

[1]Ristori, p. 13.

[2]*Ibid.*

[3]*Ibid.*

[4]*Ibid.*, p. 196.

[5]*Ibid.*, p. 188.

[6]*Ibid.*, p. IX.

[7]*Ibid.*, p. 77.

[8]*Ibid.*, p. 33.

9*Ibid.*, p. 32.

10*Ibid.*, p. 181.

11*Ibid.*, p. 19.

12*Ibid.*, p. IX.

13Henry Knepler, *The Gilded Stage: The Years of the Great International Actresses* (New York: William Morrow & Company, 1968), p. 81.

14Kennard, p. 177.

15William Winter, *Shadows of the Stage*, second series (New York: Macmillan and Company, 1893), p. 300.

16Knepler, p. 133.

17Ristori, p. 203.

18*Ibid.*, p. 128-9.

19*Ibid.*, p. 40.

20*Ibid.*, p. 70.

21*Ibid.*, p. 79.

22*Ibid.*, p. 175.

23*Ibid.*, p. 176.

24*Ibid.*, p. 142.

25Winter, p. 302.

26Ristori, p. 182.

27*Ibid.*

28*Ibid.*, p. 181.

29*Ibid.*, p. 44.

30*Ibid.*, p. 164.

31*Ibid.*, p. 165.

32*Ibid.*, p. 161.

33*Ibid.*, p. 166.

34*Ibid.*

35*Ibid.*, p. 171.

36*Ibid.*, p. 247.

37*Ibid.*, p. 171-2.

38*Ibid.*, p. 164.

39*Ibid.*, p. 51.

40*Ibid.*, p. 53.

41*Ibid.*, p. 67.

42*Ibid.*

43*New York Tribune*, September 21, 1866, p. 4.

44Edward Robins, *Twelve Great Actresses* (New York: G.P. Putnam's Sons, 1900), p. 413.

45Winter, p. 303.

46Ristori, p. 142.

47*Ibid.*, p. 141.

48*Ibid.*, p. 142.

49*Ibid.*

50*Ibid.*, pp. 158, 160.

51Robins, p. 426.

52*New York Tribune*, October 2, 1866, p. 5.

53John Ranken Towse, *Sixty Years of the Theatre* (New York: Funk and Wagnalls Company, 1916), p. 281.

54Winter, p. 302.

55Robins, p. 428.

56*Ibid.*, pp. 428-9.

57Ristori, p. 110.

58Winter, p. 301.

59Kemble, p. 246.

60Falk, p. 267.

Chapter Seven

1Sarah Bernhardt, *Memories of My Life* (New York: Benjamin Blom, 1968), p. 56.

[2]*Ibid.*, p. 38.

[3]*Ibid.*, p. 37.

[4]*Ibid.*, p. 71.

[5]*Ibid.*, p. 87.

[6]*Ibid.*, p. 83.

[7]*Ibid.*, p. 81.

[8]Sarah Bernhardt, *Art of the Theatre* (New York: Benjamin Blom, 1969), p. 116

[9]*Ibid.*

[10]Bernhardt, *Memories*, p. 104.

[11]*Ibid.*, p. 105.

[12]*Ibid.*, p. 114.

[13]Louis Verneuil, *The Fabulous Life of Sarah Bernhardt* (New York: Harper & Brothers Publishers, 1942), pp. 185-6.

[14]*Ibid.*, p. 186.

[15]*Ibid.*

[16]*Ibid.*

[17]*Ibid.*

[18]*Ibid.*

[19] Cornelia Otis Skinner, *Madame Sarah* (Boston: Houghton Mifflin Company, 1966), p. 55.

[20] Bernhardt, *Memories*, p. 134.

[21] *Ibid.*, pp. 136-7.

[22] Knepler, p. 146.

[23] Bernhardt, *Memories*, p. 139.

[24] Knepler, p. 147.

[25] Bernhardt, *Memories*, pp. 132-3.

[26] Verneuil, p. 77.

[27] Bernhardt, *Memories*, p. 240.

[28] Knepler, p. 151.

[29] Basil Woon, *The Real Sarah Bernhardt* (New York: Boni and Liveright, 1924), p. 205.

[30] Bernhardt, *Memories*, p. 266.

[31] *Ibid.*

[32] *Ibid.*, pp. 266-7.

[33] *Ibid.*, p. 267.

[34] Bernhardt, *Art*, p. 134.

[35] *Ibid.*, p. 136.

[36] May Agate, *Madame Sarah* (New York: Benjamin Blom, 1969), pp. 136-9.

[37]W. Graham Robertson, *Life was Worth Living* (New York: Harper and Brothers), p. 108.

[38]Bernhardt, *Art*, pp. 135-6.

[39]Agate, p. 139.

[40]Skinner, p. 107.

[41]Kennard, p. 132.

[42]Falk, *Rachel*, p. 181.

[43]Bernhardt, *Art*, p. 122.

[44]*Ibid.*

[45]Bernhardt, *Memories*, pp. 318-20.

[46]George Arthur, *Sarah Bernhardt* (New York: Doubleday, Page & Co., 1923), p. 76.

[47]Ellen Terry, *Ellen Terry's Memoirs* (New York: Benjamin Blom, 1969), p. 57.

[48]Lysiane Bernhardt, *Sarah Bernhardt My Grandmother* (London: Hurst and Blackett, Ltd.), p. 107.

[49]Bernhardt, *Memories*, pp. 369-70.

[50]Marion Moore Coleman, *Fair Rosalind: The American Career of Helene Modjeska* (Cheshire, CT: Cherry Hill Books, 1969), p. 158.

[51]Madame Thérèse Berton, *The Real Sarah Bernhardt* (London: Hurst & Blackett, Ltd., 1923), pp. 270-1.

[52]*Ibid.*, p. 271.

[53]Skinner, p. 166.

[54]Winter, *Wallet*, p. 500.

[55]Robertson, p. 119.

[56]Agate, p. 133.

[57]*Ibid.*, p. 131.

[58]*Ibid.*, pp. 130-1.

[59]Berton, pp. 254-5.

[60]Bernhardt, *Memories*, p. 397.

[61]Verneuil, pp. 148-9.

[62]Bernhardt, *Art*, p. 137.

[63]Lysiane Bernhardt, pp. 213-14.

[64]*Ibid.*, p. 227.

Chapter Eight

[1]Bernhardt, *Memories*, p. 343.

[2]*Ibid.*

[3]Eva Le Gallienne, *The Mystic in the Theatre: Eleonora Duse* (Carbondale, IL: Southern Illinois University Press, 1973), p. 166.

[4]*Ibid.*, p. 27.

[5]E.A. Rheinhardt, *The Life of Eleonora Duse* (New York: Benjamin Blom, 1969), pp. 17-18.

[6]William Weaver, *Duse a Biography* (New York: Harcourt Brace Jovanovich, Publishers, 1984), p. 16.

[7]Gabriele D'Annunzio, *The Flame* (The National Alumni, 1906), pp. 279-82.

[8]Weaver, pp. 35-6.

[9]*Ibid.*, p. 36.

[10]*Ibid.*, p. 37.

[11]Emma Calvé, *My Life* (New York: Arno Press, 1977), p. 60, 61.

[12]Ristori, p. 246.

[13]Weaver, p. 75.

[14]Arthur Symons, *Eleonora Duse* (New York: Benjamin Blom, 1969), p. 73.

[15]LeGallienne, pp. 101-2.

[16]Symons, p. 3.

[17]*Ibid.*, p. 69.

[18]Le Gallienne, p. 43.

[19]*Ibid.*, p. 42.

[20]Weaver, p. 89.

[21]*Ibid.*

22Archie Binns, *Mrs. Fiske and the American Theatre* (New York: Crown Publishers, Inc., 1955), p. 52.

23Weaver, p. 102.

24*Ibid.*, p. 85.

25George Bernard Shaw, *Dramatic Opinions and Essays* (New York: Brentano's 1906), pp. 129, 133.

26*Ibid.*, pp. 135-42.

27James Gordon Bennett, *New York Herald*, Paris Edition, October 10, 1987, p. 5.

28Weaver, p. 160.

29James Huneker, *Iconoclasts* (New York: Charles Scribner's Sons, 1913), p. 332.

30Terry, p. 169.

31Le Gallienne, p. 147.

32Aurelien-Marie Lugne-Poe, *La Parade: Sous Les Etoiles* (Paris: Librarie Gallinard, 1933), p. 285.

33*Ibid.*, p. 144.

34Le Gallienne, p. 80.

35Edouard Schneider, *Eleonora Duse* (Paris: Bernard Grasset, 1925), p. 164.

36Rheinhardt, p. 267.

37*Ibid.*

[38] Weaver, p. 307.

[39] *Ibid.*, p. 312.

[40] *Ibid.*, p. 317.

[41] *Ibid.*

[42] Le Gallienne, pp. 23-4.

[43] *Ibid.*, p. 24.

[44] *Ibid.*, p. 111.

[45] *Ibid.*, p. 146.

[46] *Ibid.*, pp. 153-4.

[47] Charles Chaplin, *Los Angeles Daily Times*, February 20, 1923, Section 2, pp. 1, 11.

[48] Le Gallienne, p. 68.

SELECTED BIBLIOGRAPHY

Agate, James. *Rachel*. New York: Viking Press, 1928.
Agate, May. *Madame Sarah*. New York: Benjamin Blom, 1969.
Anderson, Mary. *A Few Memories*. New York: Harper and Brothers, 1896.
Baker, H. Barton. *The London Stage: It's History and Traditions from 1576 to 1888*. London: W.H. Allen and Co., 1889.
Beauvallet, Leon. *Rachel and the New World*. New York: Abelard-Schuman, Limited, 1967.
Bernhardt, Lysiane. *Sarah Bernhardt My Grandmother*. London: Hurst and Blackette, Ltd.
Bernhardt, Sarah. *Art of the Theatre*. New York: Benjamin Blom, 1969.
Bernhardt, Sarah. *Memories of My Life*. New York: Benjamin Blom, 1968.
Binns, Archie. *Mrs. Fiske and the American Theatre*. New York: Crown Publishers, Inc., 1955.
Boswell, James. *Life of Johnson*. New York: Everyman Edition.
Browning, Robert. *Justinian and Theodora*. London: Weidenfeld and Nicolson, 1971.
Campbell, Thomas. *Life of Mrs. Siddons*. London: Effingham Wilson, 1834.
Chetwood, T. *A General History of the Stage*. London: W. Owen, 1749.
Chinoy, Helen Krich and Linda Walsh Jenkins. *Women in American Theatre, Careers, Images, Movements, An Illustrated Anthology and Sourcebook*. New York: Crown Publishers, Inc., 1981.
Cibber, Colley. *An Apology for the Life of Mr. Colley Cibber*. London: John C. Nimmo, 1889.
Clairon, Hippolyte. *Memoirs of Hippolyte Clairon*. London: G.G. and J. Robinson, 1800.
Coleman, Marion Moore. *Fair Rosalind: The American Career of Helene Modjeska*. Cheshire, CT: Cherry Hill Books, 1969.

Doty, Gresdna Ann. *The Career of Mrs. Anne Brunton Merry in the American Theatre*. Baton Rouge, LA: Louisiana State University Press, 1971.

Duerr, Edwin. *The Length and Depth of Acting*. New York: Holt Rinehart and Winston, 1962.

Dunbar, Janet. *Peg Woffington and Her World*. Boston: Houghton Mifflin Company, 1968.

Dunlap, William. *History of the American Theatre*. New York: J. and J. Harper, 1832.

Falk, Bernard. *Rachel the Immortal*. New York: Benjamin Blom, Inc., 1972.

Findlater, Richard. *The Player Queens*. New York: Taplinger Publishing Company, 1977.

Garrick, David. *The Letters of David Garrick*. Cambridge, MA: Harvard University Press, 1963.

Gilder, Rosamond. *Enter the Actress, The First Women in the Theatre*. Cambridge, MA: The Riverside Press, 1931.

Gildon, Charles. *The Life of Mr. Thomas Betterton*. London: Robert Gosling, 1710.

Huneker, James. *Iconoclasts*. New York: Charles Scribner's Sons, 1913.

Ireland, Joseph N. *Mrs. Duff*. Boston: James R. Osgood and Company, 1882.

Ireland, Joseph N. *Records of the New York Stage from 1750-1860*. New York: T.H. Morrell, 1866-67.

Joseph, Bertram. *The Tragic Actor*. London: Routledge and Kegan Paul, 1959.

Kemble, Fanny. *Records of Later Life*. New York: Henry Holt and Company, 1884.

Kemble, Frances Ann. *Records of a Girlhood*, 2nd ed. New York: Henry Holt and Company, 1884.

Kennard, Mrs. Arthur. *Rachel*. London: Witt, Allen & Co., 1885.

Knepler, Henry. *The Gilded Stage: The Years of the Great International Actresses*. New York: William Morrow & Company, 1968.

Leach, Joseph. *Bright Particular Star*. New Haven, CT: Yale University Press, 1970.

Le Gallienne, Eva. *The Mystic in the Theatre: Eleonora Duse*. Carbondale, IL: Southern Illinois University Press, 1973.

Le Gallienne, Eva. *With a Quiet Heart*. New York: The Viking Press, 1953.
Lewes, George Henry. *Dramatic Essays*. London: Walter Scott Limited, 1896.
Malpede, Karen, ed. *Women in Theatre, Compassion and Hope*. New York: Drama Book Publishers, 1983.
Manvell, Roger. *Sarah Siddons, Portrait of an Actress*. New York: G.P. Putnam's Sons, 1971.
McAfee, Helen. *Pepys on the Restoration Stage*. New York: Benjamin Blom, Inc.
Monval, Georges, ed. *Lettres de Adrienne Lecouvreur*. Paris: Librairie Plan, MDCCCXCII.
Morris, Lloyd. *Curtain Time: The Story of the American Theatre*. New York: Random House, 1953.
Odell, George C. *Annals of the New York Stage*. New York: Columbia University Press, 1927-49.
Rankin, Hugh F. *The Theatre in Colonial America*. Chapel Hill, NC: University of North Carolina Press, 1960.
Ransome, Eleanor. *The Terrific Kemble*. London: Hamish Hamilton, 1978.
Richardson, Joanna. *Rachel*. London: Max Reinhardt, 1956.
Richtman, Jack. *Adrienne Lecouvreur, The Actress and the Age*. Englewood Cliffs, NJ: Prentice-Hall, Inc., 1971.
Robertson, W. Graham. *Life was Worth Living*. New York: Harper and Brothers.
Robins, Edward. *Twelve Great Actresses*. New York: G.P. Putnam's Sons, 1900.
Ristori, Adelaide. *Memories and Artistic Studies*. New York: Benjamin Blom, 1969.
Shaw, George Bernard. *Dramatic Opinions and Essays*. New York: Brentano's, 1906.
Skinner, Cornelia Otis. *Madame Sarah*. Boston: Houghton Mifflin Company, 1966.
Sprague, A.C. *Shakespearean Players and Performances*. Cambridge, MA: Harvard University Press, 1953.
Stebbins, Emma, ed. *Charlotte Cushman, Her Letters and Memories of Her Life*. Boston: Houghton, Osgood and Company, 1878.

Symons, Arthur. *Eleonora Duse*. New York: Benjamin Blom, 1969.
Taranow, Gerda. *Sarah Bernhardt*. Princeton, NJ: Princeton University Press, 1972.
Terry, Ellen. *Ellen Terry's Memoirs*. New York: Benjamin Blom, 1969.
Towse, John Rankin. *Sixty Years of the Theatre*. New York: Funk and Wagnalls Company, 1916.
Weaver, William. *Duse a Biography*. New York: Harcourt Brace Jovanovich, Publishers, 1984.
Wilkinson, Tate. *Memoirs of His Own Life*. York: Wilson, Spence and Mawman, 1790.
Wilson, Garff B. *A History of American Acting*. Bloomington, IN: Indiana University Press, 1966.
Wilson, John Harold. *Nell Gwyn, Royal Mistress*. New York: Pellegrini & Cudahy, 1952.
Winter, William. *Other Days*. New York: Moffat, Yard and Co., 1908.
_____. *Shadows of the Stage*. New York: Macmillan and Company, 1893.
_____. *The Wallet of Time*. New York: Moffat, Yard & Co., 1913.

Index

Abbey, Henry, 148
Acacius, 3
Acte, 2
Addison, Joseph, 38
Adrienne Lecouvreur (Scribe), 96, 104-105, 112, 113, 146, 164, 177
Aelian, 2
Agar, Marie, 151-152
Agate, May, 139, 141, 149-150
Albans, Charles Beauclerk, Duke of, 32
Alcibiades (Otway), 32
Alcmène (*L'Amphitryon*, Molière), 10
Alexander the Great (Lee), 80
Alfieri, Vittorio, 109, 117, 163
Alicia (*Jane Shore*, Rowe), 76
Alixe (Prevois and Barrière), 147
Ambrosio, Arturo, 178
Amenaide (*Tancrède*, Voltaire), 24, 97
The Amorous Widow (Betterton), 29-30, 36
Anderson, Mary, 88
Ando, Flavio, 166
Andreini, Francesco, 6
Andreini, Isabella, xiii, 5-6, 125
Andromache (*The Distrest Mother*, Philips), 38, 44, 74
Andromaque (Racine), 12, 14, 97, 138
Angelica (*Love for Love*, Congreve), 35, 74

Angélique (*George Dandin*, Molière), 10
Angélique (*Le Malade imaginaire*, Molière), 10
Angelo (Hugo), 105
Anna Damby (*Kean*, Dumas *fils*), 135
Anne Boleyn (*Henry VIII*, Shakespeare), 40
Anne, Queen of England, 30
Anspach, Margrave, 25
Antony, Marc, 2
Antony and Cleopatra (Shakespeare), 166, 168
Araminta (*The Old Bachelor*, Congreve), 35
Argental, Charles - Augustin de Ferriol d', 16-19
Ariane (Corneille, Thomas), 13, 14
Aricie (*Phèdre*), 138
Armande (*Les Femmes savantes*, Molière), 10
Armani, Vicenza, 5
Arnold, Matthew, 141
Arsinoé (*Le Misanthrope*, Molière), 12
Artémire (Voltaire), 16
As You Like It (Shakespeare), 40, 43, 46
Atelina (*The Lovers*, Mountfort), 35
Athalie (Racine), 14, 134, 157
Auber, Daniel François, 130
Augustus II, King of Poland, 19

Babbitt, August, 84
Bajazet (Racine), 13, 100
Barker, James N., 83
Barnum, Phineas T., 109, 112
Baronne d'Arglade (*Le Marquis de Villemer*, Sand), 134-135
Barrett, Lawrence, 87, 89
Barrière, Théodore, 147
Barry, Elizabeth, 32-35
Barry, Spranger, 44
Barton, James, 85
Beatrice (*Much Ado About Nothing*, Shakespeare), 29, 40, 76
Beauchâteau, Mlle., 8
Beaumarchais, Pierre Augustin Caron de, 138
Beauvallet, Léon, 112
The Beaux' Stratagem (Farquhar), 37, 40, 43, 74
The Beggars Opera (Gay), 41
Behn, Aphra, 35
Béjart, Armande, 10-11
Béjart, Madeleine, 8-10, 11
Bellinda (*The Man of Mode*, Etherege), 29
Belphegor (de la Fontaine), 13
Belvidera (*Venice Preserved*, Otway), 33, 40, 46, 65, 76, 77, 80, 81, 86
Bérénice (Racine), 13
Bernhardt, Jeanne, 130
Bernhardt, Julie, 129, 130
Bernhardt, Maurice, 133-134
Bernhardt, Régina, 128, 132
Bernhardt, Rosine, 129
Bernhardt, Sarah, xiii, 126, 129-158, 159, 168, 170-174, 175, 181-182
Berthe de Savigny (*Le Sphynx*, Feuillet). 138
Berton, Pierre, 152
Berton, Thérèse, 150-151
Bertram (Simms), 80
Bertrand, Arthur, 104
Betterton, Mary Saunderson, 28-30, 70, 71
Betterton, Thomas, 29, 30, 33-34, 36
Bianca (*Fazio*, Milman), 87
Bibbiena, Bernardo Dovizi da, 5
The Bohemian Mother, 81
Boileau-Despréaux, Nicolas, 13
Boito, Arrigo, 166-167, 174, 177
Booth, Edwin, 86, 126
Booth, Junius Brutus, 80
Bouillon, Louise-Henriette-Françoise de Lorraine, Duchesse de, 19-20
Boutell, Elizabeth, 33
Boyer, 12
Bracegirdle, Anne, 30, 33-36, 37
Brontë, Charlotte, 102
Bruce, Lord, 65
Brunton, John, 76
Brutus (Payne), 80
Bulwer-Lytton, Edward, 87
Burlington, Lord, 35
Burney, Fanny, 43

Cafiero, Martino, 163
Calanthe (*Damon and Pythias*), 80
Caldwell, James H., 85
Calista (*The Fair Penitent*, Rowe), 34, 38, 40, 44, 74, 76, 77
Calvé, Emma, 165
Camille (Dumas *fils*), 148
Camille (*Horace*, Corneille), 13, 96, 97, 101, 110, 111-112

Campra, André, 22
Capranica Del Grillo, Marquis Giuliano, 117
The Careless Husband (Cibber), 34, 37, 40, 45, 74
Cato (Addison), 38
Cavalleria rusticana (Verga), 165, 175
Celia (*Volpone*, Jonson), 37
Célimène (*Le Misanthrope*, Molière), 10, 15
Cenere, 178-179
Champmeslé (Charles Chevillet), 12
Champmeslé, Marie, 11, 12-13
Chaplin, Charles, 183
Charles I, King of England, 27
Charles II, King of England, 28, 30, 31, 32
Charlotte Corday (Ponsard), 95
Chateaubriand, François René de, Vicomte de, 99
Checchi, Enrichetta, 163, 178
Checchi, Tebaldo,163, 166
Checchini, Orsola, 5
Chekhov, Anton,168, 169
Cherubin (*Le Mariage de Figaro*, Beaumarchais), 138
Chilly, Charles Marie de, 138
Chimène (*Le Cid*, Corneille), 13
Cholmondeley, Lord, 43
Cholmondeley, Captain Robert, 43
Chopin, Frédéric, 135
Choron, Étienne, 93
Churchill, Colonel Charles, 39
Cibber, Colley, 29, 34, 36, 37, 38-39, 40
Cibber, Susanna Arne, 40, 44

Cinna (Corneille), 14, 97, 101
Clairon, Claire - Josèphe - Hippolyte, 20, 21-25, 109
Claude Melnotte (*The Lady of Lyons*, Bulwer-Lytton), 87
Cléopâtre (*Rodogune*, Corneille), 20
Cléopâtre (Sardou), 153
Cleveland, Barbara Villiers, Duchess of, 32
Cleveland, Mrs. Grover, 174
Clive, Kitty, 44
Clytemnestra (*Iphigénie*, Racine), 20
Cochran, Charles Blake, 180
Coffey, Charles, 42
Coleman, Mrs. Edward, 27-28
The Comical Lovers (Cibber), 37
Congreve, William, 34, 35, 36
The Conscious Lovers (Steele), 42, 74, 76
Constance (*King John*, Shakespeare), 69
The Constant Couple (Farquhar), 41, 42, 43
Cooper, James Fenimore, 113
Cooper, Thomas A., 84
Coppée, François, 136, 153
Cordelia (*King Lear*, Shakespeare), 29, 43, 74, 76, 80, 81, 86, 134
Cordelio (*The Orphan*, Otway), 35
Coriolanus (Shakespeare), 40
Corneille, Pierre, 11, 12, 13, 14, 15, 20, 94, 96, 98, 101, 110
Corneille, Thomas, 13
Cosette (*Les Miserables*, Hugo), 160
Countess Almaviva (*The Marriage*

of Figaro, Mozart), 85
Craven, Countess of, 25
Crébillon, Prosper Jolyot de, 15, 24
Crémieux, Adolphe, 97
Crown, John, 36-37
Curll, Edmund, 32
A Cure for Covetousness or The Cheats of Scapin, 39
Cushman, Augustus, 83
Cushman, Charles, 83
Cushman, Charlotte Saunders, xiii, 83, 91
Cushman, Robert, 83
Cushman, Susan, 83
Cushman, Thomas, 83,
Custine, Adolphe, Marquis de, 99
Cytheris, 2

Damala, Jacques, 152
Daniel (Verneuil), 157
D'Angeville, Marie-Anne, 22
D'Annunzio, Gabrieli, 161-163, 174, 175-177
D'Avenant, Sir William, 28, 29, 32
De Belloy, Pierre Laurent Buirette, 24
DeBrie, Mlle., 9
Deela (*She Would be a Soldier, or the Battle of Chippewa*, Noah), 83
Delaunay, Louis, 127
Deledda, Grazia, 178
Delestre-Poirson, 95
D'eqville, James, 79
Desdemona (*Othello*, Shakespeare), 35, 40, 79
Deshais, 22
Deslandes, Raymond, 132
Desmares, Charlotte, 14

Desoeillets, Mlle., 11-13
Dickens, Charles, 87
Diderot, Denis, 21, 22
The Distrest Mother (Philips), 38, 44, 74, 76, 80
Dogget, Thomas, 37
A Doll's House (Ibsen), 169, 177
Don Sancho (Corneille), 94
Dona Maria (*Ruy Blas*, Hugo), 137
Dona Sol (*Hernani*, Hugo), 142
Dorine (*Tartuffe*, Molière), 10
The Double Falsehood (Theobold), 74
Douglas (Home), 75, 81
Douglass, David, 75
Douglass, Mrs. David (*see* Hallam, Mrs. Lewis)
Draxilla (*Alcibiades*, Otway), 32
Dryden, John, 29, 31
Dubois, 24, 25
Duchess of Malfi (Webster), 29
Duchess of York (*Richard III*, Shakespeare), 30, 75
Duclos, Marie-Anne, 14, 15
Duff, John R., 79, 82
Duff, Mary Ann Dyke, 79-83
Dumas *fils*, Alexandre, 145, 148, 163, 166, 174, 175, 177
Dumas, Alexandre *père*, 109, 117, 135
Dumesnil, Marie Françoise, xi, 20-21, 22, 23, 44
Dunlap, William, 75, 76, 78
Du Parc, Marquise - Therése, 9, 11, 12
Duport, Paul, 95
Duquesnel, Félix, 136
Duse, Alessandro, 159

Duse, Angelica, 159, 163
Duse, Eleonora, xi, 159-184
Duse, Luigi, 159
Dussane, Beatrix, 154-157

Edison, Thomas, 151, 174
Electre (Crébillon), 15, 24
Electre (Voltaire), 23
Elettra (Alfieri), 163
Élie, Georges Antoine, 131-132
Elisabeth I (*Le Comte d'Essex*, Corneille, Thomas), 13, 20
Elisabetta, regina d'Inghilterra (Giacometti), 123-125
Elise (*L'Avare*, Molière), 10
Elizabeth the Queen (Giacometti), 124
Elmire *(Tartuffe,* Molière), 10, 15
Elssler, Fanny, 109
Elvira (*The Spanish Friar*, Dryden), 29
Emilie (*Cinna*, Corneille), 14, 97, 101
Erlanger, Abe, 153
Eryphile (*Iphigénie en Aulide*, Racine), 100
Espéronnière, Antoine l', 7-8
Etherege, Sir George, 29
Euphemia, Empress, 3
Euphrasia (*The Grecian Daughter*, Murphy), 76, 77

The Fair Penitent (Rowe), 34, 35, 40, 44, 74, 77
Falstaff (Verdi), 166
Fairet, Marie, 8
Farquhar, George, 36, 37, 41
The Fatal Marriage (Southerne), 65-66
Fazio (Milman), 87
Fédora (Sardou), 152, 153
Félix, Elisa (*see* Rachel)
Félix, Esther, 93
Félix, Jacob, 93
Félix, Raphaël, 99, 109, 114
Félix, Sarah, 93, 114
Ferriol, Mme. de, 16-19
Fête de Vénus (Boyer), 12
Feuillet, Octave, 138
Fiske, Mrs. Minnie Maddern, vii, 169
Flaminia (Orsola Checchini), 5
Florimel (*The Comical Lovers*, Cibber), 37
Florimel (*Secret Love*, Dryden), 30-31
Foch, Marshal Ferdinand, 137
Foligno, Angela de, 179
Fontaine, Jean de la, 13
Forrest, Edwin, 95
Francesca da Rimini (D'Annunzio), 176
Francesca da Rimini (Pellico), 115, 117, 161
François - le - Champi (Sand), 134
Fressard, Madame, 129
Friedrich Wilhelm II, German Kaiser, 127
Frohman, Charles, 153
Fronsac, Duc de, 24
Frou-Frou (Meilhac), 164

Gainsborough, Thomas, 70
The Gamester (Moore), 40, 66, 74, 80
Garrick, David, 22-23, 36, 40, 41, 43-

44, 65, 69
Gay, John, 41
Gauthier, Théophile, 96, 103
Gazuola, Frederico de, 5
George Dandin (Molière), 10
George III, King of England, 69, 70
Gertrude (*Hamlet*, Shakespeare), 34, 40, 41, 75, 86
Giacometti, Paolo, 116, 119, 123, 124
Gilbert, John, 83
Giraud, Count Giovanni, 117
Gismondo (Sardou), 153
Goldoni, Carlo, 109
Goneril (*King Lear*, Shakespeare), 86
Gorky, Maxim, 177
The Grecian Daughter (Murphy), 76
Greeley, Horace, 81
Griffith, David Lewelyn Wark, 178
Guérin, François, 11
Guilbert, Yvette, 175
Guy Mannering (Scott), 87
Gwyn, Nell, 30-32, 100

Hallam, Lewis, 73, 74-75
Hallam, Lewis Jr., 74, 75
Hallam, Mrs. Lewis, 73-75
Hallam, William, 73
Hamlet (Shakespeare), 29, 34, 35, 40, 41, 75, 153
Harris, Augustus Glossop, 121
Hart, Charles, 30, 31
Hauptmann, Gerhart, 169
The Heart of Midlothian (Scott), 95
Hedda Gabler (Ibsen), 177
Heimat (Sudermann), 170-174, 177

Henriette (*Les Femmes savantes*, Molière), 132
Henry II, King of France, 5
Henry IV, King of France, 6
Henry IV (Shakespeare), 44
Henry VI, Part 2 (Shakespeare), 38
Henry VIII (Shakespeare), 29, 34, 40, 87
Hermione (*Andromaque*, Racine), 12-13, 14, 23, 97, 100-101
Hermione (*The Distrest Mother*, Philips), 76, 80, 81
Hernani (Hugo), 142, 146
Hesione (Campra), 22
Hofmannstahl, Hugo von, 169
Hollingshead, John, 142-143
Home, John, 75
Horace (Corneille), 13, 96, 100, 101
Horatia (*The Roman Father*, Whitehead), 76
Hugo, Victor, 97, 105, 135, 137, 142
Hyman, Al, 153

Ianthe (*The Siege of Rhodes*, D'Avenant), 28, 29
Ibsen, Henrik, 169, 177, 179
Idame (*L'Orphelin de la Chine*, Voltaire), 24
I gelosi fortunati (Giraud), 117
Ines de Castro (de La Motte), 14, 15
Il burberino benefico (Goldoni), 109
Il fuoco (D'Annunzio), 176
Il sogno d'un mattino di primavera (D'Annunzio), 175
Imogine (*Bertram*, Simms), 80
Indian Queen (*The Widow Ranter*, Behn), 35
Indiana (*The Conscious Lovers*,

Steele), 74, 76
Iphigénie (*Iphigénie en Aulide*, Racine), 13, 23, 132
Iphigénie en Aulide (Racine), 100
Ireland, Joseph N., 79, 80
Isabella (Southerne), 82
Isabella *(Don Sancho,* Corneille), 94
Isabella *(The Fatal Marriage,* Southerne), 65
Isabella *(Measure for Measure,* Shakespeare), 29
Isabella, Queen of Spain, 122-123

James I, King of England, 27
Jane Shore *(Jane Shore,* Rowe), 38, 40, 44, 74, 75, 77, 79-80, 81
Jane Shore (Rowe), 76
Janin, Jules, 95, 97-98, 109, 117
Jarrett, Edward, 145, 146, 147, 148
Jocaste *(Oedipe,* Corneille), 14
Jocasta *(Oedipus,* Dryden), 29
John Gabriel Borkman (Ibsen), 177
Johnson, Samuel, 40, 41, 43
Jonson, Ben, 37
Josephine *(La Vendéenne,* Duport), 95
Juliet *(Romeo and Juliet,* Shakespeare), 29, 74, 76, 78, 79, 87, 161-163
Justin, Roman Emperor, 2, 3
Justinian, Roman Emperor, 2-4
Juvenal (Decimus Junius Juvenalis), 2

Kean (Dumas *père*), 135
Kean, Edmund, 80
Kean, Thomas, 73

Kemble, Fanny, 82, 101, 105, 114, 127
Kemble, John Philip, 66, 70
Kemble, Robert, 46
Kemble, Sarah, 46
Kemble, Sarah (*see* Siddons, Sarah Kemble)
Kennard, Mrs. Arthur, 103, 141
Killigrew, Thomas, 28, 30
King John (Shakespeare), 69
King Lear (Shakespeare), 29, 43, 86
Klaw, Marc, 153
Kotzebue, August Friedrich Ferdinand von, 81

La Barbera, 5
La Calandria (Bibbiena), 4-5
La città morta (D'Annunzio), 176, 181-182
La Critique de L'Ecole (Molière), 10
La Czarina (Scribe), 99
La Dame aux Camélias (Dumas *fils*), 148-151, 164, 174, 175, 177
La Femme de Claude (Dumas *fils*), 175
La figlia de Jorio (D'Annunzio), 177
La Gioconda (D'Annunzio), 175, 176, 177
La gloria (D'Annunzio), 175
La Grange, 10, 11, 13
La moglie ideale (Praga), 169
La pazzia (Andreini), 6
La porta chiusa (Praga), 180, 183
Laporte, Marie Vernier, 8
La Princesse de Bagdad (Dumas *fils*), 163
La Vendéenne (Duport), 95
La Voyante, 158

Lady Anne (*Richard III*, Shakespeare), 40, 65, 74
Lady Betty Modish (*The Careless Husband*, Cibber), 37, 38-39, 40, 45, 74
Lady Brute (*The Provoked Wife*, Vanbrugh), 39, 40, 43
Lady Easy (*The Careless Husband*, Cibber), 34
The Lady from the Sea (Ibsen), 177, 179
Lady Jane Gray (*Lady Jane Gray*, Rowe), 38
Lady Leycock (*The Amorous Widow*, Betterton), 29-30
Lady Macbeth (*Macbeth*, Shakespeare), 29, 34, 40, 46-64, 67-68, 70, 78, 80, 83, 85-86, 87, 88, 121-122, 123, 125-126, 179
Lady Macduff (*Macbeth*, Shakespeare), 40
The Lady of Lyons (Bulwer-Lytton), 87
Lady Percy (*Henry IV*, Shakespeare), 44, 74
Lady Randolph (*Douglas*, Home), 75, 81
Lady Townley (*The Provoked Husband*, Cibber), 38, 45, 74
L'Aiglon (Rostand), 153
L'Amphitryon (Molière), 10
L'Avare (Molière), 10
Lavinia (*The Fair Penitent*, Rowe), 35
Lawrence, Thomas, 70
Le Bourgeois gentilhomme (Molière), 10
Lebrun, Charles François, 101

Le Cid (Corneille), 13
Le Comte d'Essex (Corneille, Thomas), 13, 20
Le conte, Valleran, 8
Lecouvreur, Adrienne, xiii, 14-20, 22, 96, 109
Le Docteur amoureux (Molière), 9-10
Lee, Nathaniel, 33, 38, 80
Le Gallienne, Eva, 159, 176, 180-182, 184
Legouvé, Ernest, 104-105, 117, 120
Le Grand, 15
Lejay, Mme., 15
Leke, Robert, Earl of Scarsdale, 36
Le Malade imaginaire (Molière), 11
Le Marquis de Villemer (Sand), 134
Le Misanthrope (Molière), 10, 12, 15
Leonora (*Sir Courtly Nice*, Crown), 36
Le Passant (Coppée), 136
Les Femmes savantes (Molière), 10, 132
Les Miserables (Hugo), 160
Le Siège de Calais (DeBelloy), 24
Le Sphynx (de Savigny), 138
L'Etrangère (Dumas *fils*), 145, 146
Lewes, George Henry, 103, 114
Ligne, Prince Henri de, 133-134
Lillo, George, 74
L'Impromptu de Versailles (Molière), 10
Lincoln, Mary Todd, 146-147
Lind, Jenny, 109, 112
Lohman, Helen, 182
The London Merchant (Lillo), 74
Longpierre, Bernard de

Rogueleyne, 20, 24
Lorenzaccio (de Musset), 153
L'Orphelin de la Chine (Voltaire), 23, 24
Louis Philippe, King of France, 98, 106
Louis XIV, King of France, 9, 10, 11
Love for Love (Congreve), 34, 35, 74
Loveit (*A Cure for Covetousness or The Cheats of Scapin*), 39
The Lovers (Mountfort), 35
The Lower Depths (Gorky), 177
Lucile (*Le Bourgeois gentilhomme*, Molière), 10
Lugné-Poë, Aurélien-Marie, 177

Macbeth (Shakespeare), 40, 41
Macheath (*The Beggar's Opera*, Gay), 41
Macready, William, 64, 66, 71, 83, 87, 118
Madame Delancour (*Il burberino benefico*, Goldoni), 109
Maeder, James G., 85
Maffei, Andrea, 117
Magda (*Heimat*, Sudermann), 170-174, 175
Mahomet (Voltaire), 76
Mahomet and Irene (Johnson), 40
The Man of Mode (Etherege), 29
Mantua, Duke of, 6
Marchionni, Carlotta, 115
Marcia (*Cato*, Addison), 38
Marenco, Carlo, 116
Margaret (*Henry VI, Part 2*), 38
Marguerite Gauthier (*La Dame aux Camélias*, Dumas fils), 148-151, 164, 169, 175

Margherita, Queen Mother of Italy, 127
Maria (*The London Merchant*, Lillo), 74
Maria Antonietta (Giacometti), 116, 119
Maria Stuarda (*Maria Stuarda*, Maffei), 117
Maria Stuart (Schiller), 118, 126
Mariamne (*Mariamne*, Voltaire), 16
Marie Louise, French Empress, 153
Marie Stuart (*Marie Stuart*, Lebrun), 101
Mariette (*François-le-Champi*, Sand), 134
Marmontel, Jean François, 23
The Marriage of Figaro (Mozart), 85
Mars, Mlle., 97
Marshall, Anne, 28
Mary, Queen of England, 30
Mary (*Superstition*, Barker), 83
Mascagni, Pietro, 165
Mathilde (*The Bohemian Mother*), 81
Mattocks, Isabella Hallam, 74
Maynwaring, Sir Arthur, 39
McCullough, John, 90
Measure for Measure (Shakespeare), 29
Medea (Legouvé), 105, 117, 120-121
Medea (*Medea*, Longpierre), 20, 24
Médici, Cathérine de, 5, 8
Médici, Marie de, 6, 8
Meggs, Mary, 30
Meg Merrilies (*Guy Mannering*, Scott), 87

Meilhac, Henri, 164
Mendelssohn, Robert von, 179
The Merchant of Venice
(Shakespeare), 43, 65, 74
Merope (*Merope*, Voltaire), 20
Merry, Ann Brunton, 75-79
Merry, Robert, 77
The Merry Wives of Windsor,
(Shakespeare), 34
Metamora (Stone), 83
Millamant (*The Way of the World*,
Congreve), 35, 45
Milman, Henry Hart, 87
Milton, John, 46, 70
Miranda (*The Tempest*,
Shakespeare), 74
Mirtilla (Andreini), 6
Mithridate (Racine), 23, 100
Mithridates (Lee), 38
Mlle. de Belle Isle (*Mlle. de Belle Isle*, Dumas père), 138
Mme. Delancour (*Il burberino benefico*, Goldoni), 109
Modène, Esprit-Rémond de Moirmoiron, Baron de, 9
Molière (Jean-Baptiste Poquelin), 9-11, 12, 94, 132, 145
Moncalvo, Giuseppi, 115
Monime (*Mithridate*, Racine), 23, 100
Monimia (*The Orphan*, Otway), 33, 37, 76, 77
Montrin, Ada, 135
Montvoisin, Cathérine, 12
Moore, Edward, 40, 66
Morny, Charles Auguste Louis Joseph, Duc de, 130, 132
Morris, Clara, 147-148

Motte, Antoine Houdard de La, 14
Mountfort, William, 35
Mozart, Wolfgang Amadeus, 85
Mrs. Alving (*Ghosts*, Ibsen), 180
Mrs. Beverley (*The Gamester*, Moore), 40, 66, 74, 80
Mrs. Brittle (*The Amorous Widow*, Betterton), 36
Mrs. Fainall (*Love for Love*, Congreve), 34
Mrs. Ford (*The Merry Wives of Windsor*, Shakespeare), 34
Mrs. Haller (*The Stranger*, Kotzebue), 81, 86
Mrs. Marwood (*The Way of the World*, Congreve), 34
Mrs. Sullen (*The Beaux' Stratagem*, Farquhar), 37, 40, 43, 74
Much Ado About Nothing
(Shakespeare), 29, 40, 76
Murphy, Arthur, 76
Murray, Walter, 73
Musset, Alfred de, 135, 153
Myrrha (Alfieri), 118
Myrrha (*Myrrha*, Alfieri), 109, 117
Mystery of St. Catherine, 7

Nameokee (*Metamora*, Stone), 83
Nancy Sykes (*Oliver Twist*, Dickens), 87
Napoléon I, French Emperor, 153
Napoléon III, French Emperor, 104, 136, 137
Nathalie, Mme., 132
Nero, Roman Emperor, 2
Nerissa (*The Merchant of Venice*, Shakespeare), 43
Nicholas I, Czar of Russia, 107

Nixon, Sam, 153
Noah, Mordecai, M., 83
Noailles, Duc and Duchesse de, 99
Nora (*A Doll's House*, Ibsen), 169, 177

Oedipe (Corneille), 14
Oedipe (Voltaire), 19
Oedipus (Dryden), 29
The Old Bachelor (Congreve), 35
Oldfield, Anne, 20, 36-39
Oliver Twist (Dickens), 87
O'Neill, James, 89
Ophelia (*Hamlet*, Shakespeare), 29, 35, 42, 77, 79, 80, 81, 86, 163
Oreste (Voltaire), 23
Orléans, Philippe de France, Duc D', 9-10
The Orphan (Otway), 33, 35, 37, 76, 77
Otello (Verdi), 166
Othello (Shakespeare), 35, 40
Otway, Thomas, 32, 33, 35

Paddon, William, 84
Palmira (*Mahomet*, Voltaire), 76
Paulina (*Thomaso*, Killigrew), 30
Pauline (*Polyeute*, Corneille), 14
Payne, John Howard, 80
Pellico, Silvio, 115, 161
Pepys, Samuel, 31
Perdita (*The Winter's Tale*, Shakespeare), 76
Perrin, Emile, 138, 142, 143
Phèdre (*Phèdre*, Racine), 22, 23, 102-103, 110, 139-142, 143-145
Phèdre (Racine), 13, 19, 138, 143
Philips, Ambrose, 38

Phillis (*The Conscious Lovers*, Steele), 42
Pia dei Tolomei (Marenco), 116
Pinero, Sir Arthur Wing, 177
Piozzi, Hester Lynch Thrale, 65
Pirandello, Luigi, 164
Plautus, Titus Maccius, 4, 5
Polly Peachum (*The Beggar's Opera*, Gay), 41
Polyeute (Corneille), 15, 114
Ponsard, François, 95
Poquelin, Jean-Baptiste (*see* Molière)
Portia (*The Merchant of Venice*, Shakespeare), 65, 74
Portsmouth, Louise Reneé de Kerouaille, Duchess of, 32
Powell, Mrs., 84
Procopius, 3
Provost, Jean-Baptiste, 94, 131
Praga, Marco, 169, 180
Prevois, Baroness de, 147
Primoli, Count Giuseppi, 161
Princesse Dimchinka (*Un Mari qui lance sa femme*, Deslandes), 133
Pritchard, Hannah, 39-41, 44, 67
Pitchard, William, 41
The Provoked Husband (Cibber), 38, 45, 74
The Provoked Wife (Vanbrugh), 39, 40, 43
Psyché (*Psyché*, Corneille, Molière, Quinault), 11

Queen Anne (*Richard III*, Shakespeare), 35
Queen Elizabeth (*Elisabetta, regina d'Inghilterra*, Giacometti), 123-125

Queen Katherine (*Henry VIII*, Shakespeare), 29, 34, 81, 87
Quinault, Phillippe, 11

Rachel (Elisa Félix), xiii, 93-114, 115, 118, 125, 129, 132, 139, 140, 141
Racine, Jean Baptiste, 12, 15, 20, 23, 94, 97, 100, 102, 110, 132, 134, 138, 139, 157
Récamier, Jeanne Françoise Julie Adélaïde, Mme., 99
The Recruiting Officer (Farquhar), 37, 42
Régine Armand (Verneuil), 157
Regnier, François Joseph Pierre, 131, 139
Reilleux, Matilda I., 83
Reinagle, Alexander, 78
Réjane (Gabrielle Charlotte Reju), 175
Reynolds, Sir Joshua, 70
Rich, Christopher, 33, 36, 37
Rich, John, 43
Richard III (Shakespeare), 30, 35, 40, 65, 75
Ristori, Adelaide, 109-111, 115-127, 145, 159, 165-166
Ristori, Antonio, 115
Ristori, Maddalena Pomatelli, 115
The Rival Queens (Lee), 33, 35
Robertson, Graham, 149
Rochester, John Wilmot, Earl of, 32-33
Rodoqune (Corneille), 20
The Roman Father (Whitehead), 76
Romeo (*Romeo and Juliet*, Shakespeare), 87
Romney, George, 70

Rosalind (*As You Like It*, Shakespeare), 40, 43, 45, 46
Rosmersholm (Ibsen), 177
Ross, Madame, 30
Rossi, Cesare, 163, 170
Rostand, Edmond, 153
Rousseil, Roselia, 139
Rowe, Nicholas, 34, 35, 38
Roxana (*Alexander the Great*, Lee), 80
Roxane (*Bajazet*, Racine), 13, 100
Ruy Blas (Hugo), 135, 137, 138

Sackville, Charles, Earl of Dorset, 31
Saint-Aulaire, Pagnon, 93
Salle, Jouslin de la, 94
Salvini, Tommaso, 127
Samson, Joseph Isidore, 94, 95-96, 97, 99, 102, 131
Sand, George, 134-135
Santuzza (*Cavalleria rusticana*, Verga), 165
Sarcey, Francisque, 132, 137, 141, 175
Sardou, Victorien, 152-153, 166
Savoy, Duke of, 6
Saxe, Maréchal Maurice de, 19
Scala, Flaminio, 6
Schiller, Friedrich, 118, 126
Scott, Sir Walter, 87, 95
Scribe, Augustin Eugene, 96, 99, 132, 148, 177
Seaver, Joel G., 82-83
The Second Mrs. Tanqueray (Pinero), 177
Selima (*Tamerlane*, Rowe), 35
Sémiramis (*Sémiramis*, Voltaire),

21
Shakespeare, William, 29, 30, 35, 40, 44, 46, 69, 70, 134, 153, 166-167
Shaw, George Bernard, 170-174
She Would Be A Soldier, or the Battle of Chippewa (Noah), 83
Sheridan, Richard Brinsley, 65, 67-68
Siddons, Sarah Kemble, xi, xiii, 46-71, 73, 76-77, 78, 81, 88, 122
Siddons, William, 46, 70
The Siege of Rhodes (D'Avenant), 27-28, 29
Silvia (*The Recruiting Officer*, Farquhar), 37, 42, 43
Simms, William Gilmore, 80
Sir Courtly Nice (Crown), 36-37
Sir Harry Wildair (*The Constant Couple*, Farquhar), 41, 42, 43
Skinner, Cornelia Otis, 148
The Spanish Friar (Dryden), 29
Sophonisba (*Sophonisba*, Thomson), 38
Southerne, Thomas, 65, 82
Statira (*The Rival Queens*, Lee), 35
Stebbins, Emma, 89
Steele, Sir Richard, 42
Stone, John A., 83
The Stranger (Kotzebue), 81, 86
Stuart, Gilbert, 70
Sudermann, Hermann, 170, 175, 177
Superstition (Noah), 83
Swiney, Owen, 37

Taafe, 42
Talbot, Denis-Stanislas, 131
Talma, François Joseph, 96

Tamerlane (Rowe), 35
Tancrède (Voltaire), 24, 97
Tartuffe (Molière), 10, 15
Tasso, Torquato, 6
The Tempest (Shakespeare), 74
Tenison, Dr. Thomas, 32
Terence (Publius Terentius Afer), 5
Terry, Ellen, 145, 176
Theobald, Lewis, 74
Theodora, Roman Empress, xi, 2-4
Théodora (Sardou), 153
Thérèse Raquin (Zola), 163
Thierry, Edouard, 132
Thomaso (Killigrew), 30
Thomson, James, 38
Tisbé (*Angelo*, Hugo), 105-106
Tosca (Sardou), 153, 154
Towse, John Ranken, 125
Tullia (*Brutus*, Payne), 80
Twelfth Night (Shakespeare), 29
Tyrranic Love (Dryden), 31

Un Mari qui lance sa femme (Deslandes), 132

Valeria (*Tyrannic Love*, Dryden), 31
Valérie (*Valérie*, Scribe), 132
Vanbrugh, George, Sir, Captain, 36, 39
Vandenhoff, George, 86
Venice Preserved (Otway), 33, 46, 68, 77, 80, 86
Vénus (*Fête de Vénus*, Boyer), 12
Vénus (*Hesione*, Campra), 22
Verbruggen, Susanna, 36
Verdi, Giuseppi, 166
Verga, Giovanni, 165
Verneuil, Louis, 151, 157

Véron, Dr. Louis - Désiré, 104
Victor Emmanuel III, King of Italy, 127
Victoria, Queen of England, 101-102, 170
Villette (Brontë), 102
Viola (*Twelfth Night*, Shakespeare), 29
Violante (*The Double Falsehood*, Theobald), 74
Violante, Mme., 41, 42
Volpone (Jonson), 37
Voltaire (François-Marie Arouet), 16, 20, 21, 23, 24, 38, 76, 97, 138
Volumnia (*Coriolanus*, Shakespeare), 40

Walewski, Count Alexander, 104
Walpole, Horace, Earl of Oxford, 36
Warren, William, 78
Wassilissa (*The Lower Depths*, Gorky), 177
The Way of the World (Congreve), 34, 35, 45
Webster, John, 29
Whitehead, William, 76
Whitlock, Elizabeth Kemble, 73
The Widow Ranter (Behn), 35
Wignell, Thomas, 78
Wilhelm Friedrich I, German Kaiser, 136
Wilkinson, Tate, 45
Wilks, Robert, 37
Winter, William, 86, 90, 118, 125, 126-127, 148-149
The Winter's Tale (Shakespeare), 76
Woffington, Margaret, xi, 39, 41-46

Woffington, Polly, 43
Wood, Joseph, 85
Wood, Mary Ann, 85

Young, Charles, 82

Zacconi, Ermete, 179
Zacharie (*Athalie*, Racine), 134
Zaïre (*Zaïre*, Voltaire), 138
Zanetto (*Le Passant*, Coppée), 136, 153
Zénobie (*Rhadamiste et Zénobie*, Crébillon), 24
Zimmerman, Fred, 153
Zola, Emile, 163